LEVEL UP YOUR LIFE AND CAREER

Learn How to Analyze People through Human Psychology, Body Language and Personality Types

NATHAN POWELL

TABLE OF CONTENTS

Introduction 1

CHAPTER 1: HOW TO ACCURATELY AND
QUICKLY ANALYZE PEOPLE 5

CHAPTER 2: HOW TO HANDLE OBJECTIONS AND
RESISTANCE 14

CHAPTER 3: HOW TO READ NON-VERBAL CUES
....29

CHAPTER 4: THE DIFFERENT PERSONALITY
TYPES... 40

CHAPTER 5: ADVANCED HUMAN PSYCHOLOGY52

CHAPTER 6: READING BASIC BODY LANGUAGE59

CHAPTER 7: THE POWER OF THE HANDSHAKE 71

CHAPTER 8: USING EYE SIGNALS THE RIGHT
WAY 84

CHAPTER 9: THE QUICKEST WAY TO BUILD
RAPPORT 97

CHAPTER 10: ADVANCED FORMS OF BODY LANGUAGE READING 110

CHAPTER 11: THE EASIEST WAY TO BUILD CHARISMA 118

CHAPTER 12: DEALING WITH OBJECTIONS 133

CHAPTER 13: HOW TO WIN ARGUMENTS 140

CHAPTER 14: DETECTING LIES AND DECEPTION 153

CONCLUSION 167

REFERENCES 169

Introduction

There is a growing need to understand the people we interact with on a daily basis. From business associates to employees, colleagues, clients, and prospects – these people virtually form our professional world. It stands to reason that since most of our productive adult lives are spent with these groups of people, it is necessary to understand how to improve our relationship with them in order to give our businesses or careers a boost.

However, with the very many complexities that are associated with human behavior, understanding the many different individuals in our professional lives is a very daunting task for a lot of people. And as if that is not difficult enough, the pace at which technology is affecting human interaction makes our people-reading skills less sharp. Technology has produced a lot of online communication "experts" who cannot even maintain eye contact with a stranger in real life, let alone observe them long enough to accurately read their body language.

There are those who have long wished to learn the basics they need to improve their communication skills in order to have the upper hand in their interactions with clients and prospects. But the challenge of going through the series of courses required to study human psychology is a challenge they would rather not take on due to several reasons. Others too have found that they have to deal with difficult people in the workplace and that can be very challenging and draining. It is like sucking the life out of them each time they have to make contact with such difficult people.

In this book, I have taken the time to outline, in simple terms, the skills, steps, and tips that will help you improve your ability to both read people and also to effectively handle them. What you need to know about body language, human psychology, and how personality affects business are all presented in an easy-to-understand manner. If you have difficulty knowing how to marry people's words with their body language, this book will expose you to that particular knowledge. You will also get to learn how to show others that you see things from their unique point of view.

There is no denying the fact that your business and career is bound to improve if you have a strong rapport with clients, employees, and employers. I have included herein, the necessary steps to build a long-lasting rapport with the people that matter most to you especially in a professional setting.

There are many times when our lack of understanding of the way the human mind works and of glaring sings expressed by nonverbal cues will allow us to continue to direct our efforts at people who are least interested in us or what we have to offer. In this book, you will discover how to know if someone you are talking to is showing signs of interest or disinterest. You will also learn how to effectively handle objections and use them to your advantage.

The very basics of putting forward your best self in any meeting or interaction including first-time meetings are also covered in this book.

WHO THIS BOOK IS FOR

This book is specifically targeted at the business owner or employer who intends to further understand their employees' mindset with the aim of improving their business. If you really want to know the meaning behind those hand gestures and foot movements during meetings, this book is for you.

For the salesperson or marketer who looks forward to improving his or her rapport-building techniques, this book is also written for you. You will understand when a prospect is likely to raise objections or resistance and learn how to quickly use this knowledge to your advantage. This will all translate into more sales for you.

Employees who want to improve their standing with their employers or bosses will also find a great deal of information that will be beneficial for them in this book. Your career is set for the next level if you implement the ideas spelled out in this book. You will enjoy enhanced relationships with bosses, subordinates, and colleagues alike.

Although the focus of this book is on business and career, you can also use the knowledge to improve your social relationship with family and friends.

In general, this book is written for anyone who truly desires to enhance the quality of the relationship they have with other people.

CHAPTER 1:

HOW TO ACCURATELY AND QUICKLY ANALYZE PEOPLE

"The way we communicate with others and with ourselves ultimately determines the quality of our lives." (Tony Robbins, 1960, Entrepreneur, Author, and Motivational Speaker)

We live in a world where people say one thing and mean another. It is apparent that getting to the root of what people really mean will require more than just listening to words that are spoken. People are generally predictable if we know how to read them. This is why developing the skills to hear what is said and unsaid is vital to analyzing the people we interact with on a daily basis whether in a social or professional setting.

For our business and social lives to improve, we need to up our communication skills both verbally and nonverbally. It is a lot easier to listen to someone speak and understand what they mean. Decoding body language, on the other hand, is a bit tricky because they are not 100% straightforward. And as a matter of fact, there are those who can successfully hide their body language and make it even more difficult to know their intent. Nevertheless, when you master the art of reading body language, you can tell when someone is trying to hide involuntary nonverbal cues.

One of the very first steps in analyzing people is reading between the lines of their words – not with the aim of construing it, but with the aim of understanding them better and possibly relating with them better. Therefore, if you desire a good working relationship even with the most difficult person in your company, you need to first understand them by studying their body language, knowing what they are not saying, and hearing what they mean instead of what they say.

Some of the things to look out for when trying to quickly analyze people in any situation are fidgeting, uneasiness, facial expressions, and moods. Ask yourself what their body posture is like. Are they on the edge of their seat? Is the conversation in a conspiratorial or hushed tone? Do they stop talking when someone walks by or steps into the room? These are some of the things and questions that hold the clue to deeper meanings beyond mere words.

In relating with colleagues, bosses, clients, prospects, and customers you will encounter different nonverbal cues that give a clear insight into the minds of the people you interact with. But if you do not know how to read these nonverbal cues, you are simply dealing or relating to the superficial part of people. And of course, your relationship with them will be as shallow as your understanding of them.

If you see anyone who seems to get along with every other person and seems to be more successful in passing along his or her ideas, products, or services, they probably have a good understanding of their clients, colleagues, bosses, or prospects. You see, it is not merely how well-read you are in your chosen field, or how many years of experience you have in your career that makes all the difference. If you want to excel at relating to people and by extension improve your quality of job output, good knowledge of how to read people is indispensable.

Let us now consider some skills you need to master in order to be able to read and analyze people.

THE 7 STEPS TO READING PEOPLE

One: Make Personal Contact

Making friends, meeting people, and communicating with others have been made a lot easier with technology. Now we can even relate to people who are even on the other side of the world without even stepping out of bed. However, the same technology that has made communication easier has become one of the greatest obstacles to personal contact with the people in our lives.

From family to friends, to even business associates, we can send emails, texts, faxes, make calls, or even hold a conference call without the need to physically be in the same location. And with this, we have gradually lost our people-reading skills. Face-to-face communication is quite different from other forms of communication. In face-to-face communication, you can gauge people's reaction, marry it with the tone of their voice, and draw an informed conclusion. For example, if you need a favor from a colleague, you could simply walk up to them and ask. They may gladly say yes and you can see it from their eyes that they want to help, or, they may say yes but from the look on their face you can tell it is not convenient for them or they are not really willing to do it. In short, there are a lot of possible combinations of meanings that can be deduced in face-to-face communication. If, however, you choose to simply send your colleague a text message on their phone, you will only get a response that contains only the facts. You miss out on all the other nonverbal cues that could convey a completely different message from their response.

The very first skill to develop is making physical personal contact with people. Liking someone on social media is different from liking them in person. So, get in the habit of knocking on your neighbor's door and having a real conversation about the kids instead of just conversing over the phone. Learn to walk up to people and compliment them in person instead of just clicking buttons that do the same on social media. Chat up real people in real life instead of chatting them up on the internet.

My point is, re-engage your people-reading abilities as much as possible. With continuous practice, you will only get better.

Two: Observe

Reading people is not as easy as reading the words in a book. The words don't change; you do not need to observe them. They always say the same thing. However, with people, one gesture could mean several things. For example, a smile could mean a friendly disposition, and that same person could give another smile that could mean a disdain or even anger – same person, same facial expression, but a different meaning.

This is why it takes patience to be able to accurately read people. You need to observe the words spoken and how it is spoken as well as what tone of voice is used. Observe how they sigh or shift their weight from one foot to the other or how and when they fidget around in a chair. Observe if they are tapping their fingers or if they are squinting their eyes. All these are clues tell you what is going on with them in a particular context.

You do not need to immediately form an opinion about one particular gesture. All you need to do first is to get in contact with people and then observe their general behavior. Take the time to form what is known as a baseline for their normal behavior or body language. It is when you have determined to a fair extent the baseline of a person that you can accurately read that particular individual. And this happens when you notice a deviation from their usual or normal body language.

Three: Open Up

Communication usually works best when in it done from both ends. In other words, it is a two-way street. If you want other people to open up to you, you definitely have to open up to them as well. It is only natural that if people feel they can read you to some extent, then they too will be willing to let down their guard so you can read them. It is like giving them a glimpse of yourself so that you can get a clearer view of them.

When you truly want to build rapport, you have to be forthcoming about your views as well. Saying things that are politically correct or things that are expected will only get you half-hearted responses. By all means, be honest. This is the best way to get others to be downright open with you as well.

Four: Know Exactly What You Want

You must determine what it is you are looking for in a person or else you may find that you will be disappointed in the long run. What type of business partner or client are you looking for? What are the qualities that will make them the ideal partners to work with? When you have your preferences written down or mentally figured out, it becomes easy to compare real-life people with your list to see if they match.

Five: Be Objective

Perhaps one of the most difficult of all the people-reading skills is being objective. The truth is, you cannot effectively or accurately read people if you are not looking at them from an objective perspective. It is more difficult to be truly objective if you have to read people in whom you have vested interest. For example, it may not take too much consideration for you to fire a new employee, but when you have an employee that has a long-standing relationship with you it becomes difficult to be objective when analyzing their behavior even if it is hurting your company.

There is a tendency for us to be less objective when a decision is important to us. Nevertheless, if your people-reading skills are going to be anywhere near accurate, you have to remain focused on the task at hand.

For you to stay focused on your objectiveness, you must learn to overcome emotional attachments and fear of making decisions.

Six: Start Fresh

Accurately reading people means you have decided to drop all preconceived notions and prejudices about them. You are ready to start anew to evaluate every sign based on its own merit. In other words, you are dropping all prejudices about sex, appearance, race, age, financial status, etc. It is very erroneous to form an opinion about an individual based on a predisposition you have about people with a certain characteristic. That would be blindly stereotyping people and not even close to accurately reading them.

Begin to acknowledge your prejudices and your biases and drop them one after the other. This is the way to start fresh. This cleans up your slate and allows you to evaluate with a clear mind.

Seven: Decide and Take Action

Once you have evaluated or analyzed a person, decide what to do with your evaluation and take action. There is no point putting in the effort to create behavior baseline, read body language, juxtapose them with spoken words to know if they are conveying the same message, and after all the analyzing and evaluating do not take any action on the conclusion of the analysis.

If you have judged a person to be reliable, by all means, strengthen your rapport with them. If they are sloppy, dishonest, or cunning, then there is no likely point in maintaining the relationship.

Taking action (no matter how difficult it may appear), is the most sensible thing to do after analyzing people. Make decisions and act upon your evaluation to advance your career, build stronger relationships, and improve your business relations.

CHAPTER 2:

HOW TO HANDLE OBJECTIONS
AND RESISTANCE

"An objection is not a rejection; it is simply a request for more information." (Bo Bennett, 1972, Businessman)

Objections and resistance are common occurrences in everyday life and particularly in the business world. Ignorantly, some salespersons view objections as a terrible thing. But which is worse: having a client say "no thanks" without taking a look at your offer, or listening and raising objections? I bet you will agree with me that outright rejection is worse. When someone raises an objection, it is very likely that all they need is some clarification before they accept your offer.

In order to effectively handle objections or resistance, you must first shift your perception from seeing objection as bad to seeing it as an indication of some underlying concerns or issues which when resolved, can bring about the result you seek. And even if it does not produce the desired effect with the client that raised the objection, you would have learned how to better present your offer with your next client.

Objections basically signify that the other person requires more information, wants their doubts cleared, or they need more assurance. Not everyone expresses objections in the same way. Some object or resist openly, others imply it, while some others try to hide it. While it is fairly easy to handle open and implied objections, it requires a certain level of expertise to identify a hidden objection. This is where a good knowledge of body language comes to play.

If you simply ignore an objection or if you cannot recognize when a prospect is raising an objection, you probably won't sell any of your ideas or products at least to that particular prospect. You should either address the objections once they are raised, or anticipate objections and trash them before they are even raised. To successfully close a deal, you must know how to effectively handle objections.

In this chapter, we shall take a look at a few examples of common objections, how to effectively deal with them, and proven techniques that can help you handle objections in specific scenarios.

TYPICAL OBJECTIONS AND RESISTANCE

If you can identify an objection or resistance you are a lot closer to effectively handle it. Here are the most common types of objections you are likely to face.

Source

This objection may be misconstrued as a personal attack on you, but it is usually not so. Your potential buyer will question the authenticity and credibility of your product or service, and sometimes, they may also want to ask you personal questions. For example:

"Why should I trust you? I don't know you."

"I have a reliable customer already."

"How come I've not heard about your company until now?"

Need

This type of objection tends to sway more towards rejection. The prospect says they have no need for your service or product. For example:

"I have something similar already."

"I don't think I need this."

Features

This objection is a very positive response. As a matter of fact, when you notice this, you have done a good job of pitching or presenting. This objection comes in response to aspects of the details of a product or a service you are offering. It simply means they are considering your offer but need clarification. For example:

"The technology is a bit outdated."

"The guarantee period is too short."

"Is there no way to make this smaller?"

Time

This type of objection is centered on it not being the right time to make a purchase or to buy into an idea. For example:

"I think I need more time to think about this."

"Perhaps I'll have enough money for this by next month."

"Maybe I'll get back to you after consulting with my partners."

Price

This is a very common type of objection, although many prospects will not directly broach the topic. It usually is a hidden objection for many people, but if you dig deeper, you will uncover it. Typically, price objections come up in statements like:

"I didn't budget for this."

"I can get it cheaper elsewhere."

"And this does not include service fee?"

All these may sound like a "no" but they are natural responses you should expect from someone who does not know exactly what it is you offer. That is why you need to know how to handle these objections and use them as stepping stones to close your deal.

6 STEPS TO EFFECTIVELY HANDLE OBJECTIONS

Step 1: Listen

The first step in handling objections is to listen to what the other person is objecting about. And when I say listen, I mean hear what they are saying and also what they are not saying by paying attention to their body language. Cutting your prospect short in the middle of their objection may turn them off. Allow them to say exactly what it is that they are concerned about. Your goal is not to give a textbook answer, but to first understand their perspective and then see how best you can help them see another point of view.

Step 2: Summarize their Concerns

When you are sure your client or prospect has finished talking, allow a few seconds to pause before you start responding. In those few seconds, you should not just appear thoughtful, but actually think about their objections and the best method to use in handling the objection. Now, summarize the major points of their concerns in a few short sentences. You can begin by saying something along the lines of, *"So, if I get you correctly, you are saying…"* then repeat what they have said succinctly so that they can confirm or clarify. This shows the client that you actually paid attention to them.

Step 3: Dig Deeper

When a clear objection has been established through confirmation or clarification, you can ask them to tell you more about this concern they have. Most times, people do not start with their major objection, but using this approach may give them the nudge to delve deep and bring up more objections or even bring up the main concern they have. So, take a few moments to dig deeper through explorative questions like, *"aside from this concern, what other aspect are you not comfortable with?"* or *"in what ways has this posed a problem for you in time past?"* This shows the client or prospect that you are genuinely concerned about resolving their objections.

Your aim at this point should be to dig up the hidden or major objection; therefore, the longer time you spend on this phase of handling objections, the higher your chances of getting to the root of the concern.

Step 4: Address the Objection

Now it is time to address the objection directly. Remember that your prospect or client is objecting because they need clarification, more information, or reassurance – basically, they are expressing fear. So, when you address their objections, you are not merely defending your idea or product, but you are also removing their fears and doubts. Instead of a defensive attitude, take a stance of empathy. You connect more with them when you empathize instead of defending.

In addressing objections you can use concrete pieces of evidence to clear doubts and assuage fears. Share real-life stories if you have them. Refer to other customers' positive experiences if you have any. Give current verifiable statistics if you have some. In general, you should give evidence that can be verified independently, preferably online such as on websites that are not affiliated to yours (if available).

Step 5: Confirm that Objections are Cleared

After addressing the objection, be sure to check if you have cleared the objection. You can simply ask, *"Does this answer your question?"* or something along that line. If they confirm it has, you can proceed to the final step, if not; you can back up to an earlier step and repeat the process. Sometimes, the prospect may not categorically say they are not satisfied with your answer but if you can read body language, you should be able to pick up any sign of hesitation. In such case, simply say something like, *"I think we should go back, and see if we can make this clearer."*

Step 6: Pick Up Where You Left Off

It is time to return to where you were before the objection was raised. If it was in the middle of your presentation or pitch, simply summarize what you have said earlier and redirect the conversation to continue from where you left off. If it was at the end of your pitch or presentation you can begin the closing process.

TECHNIQUES FOR HANDLING OBJECTIONS

There are several techniques you can adopt when you address objections. Let us consider a few of these techniques.

The Boomerang

Knowing how to use this technique effectively will almost always guarantee a sale or acceptance. It involves turning an objection or an argument around to your advantage.

For example:

"I see you do not have the money now, but we could work out a payment plan."

"I totally agree that it is quite expensive, but your company shouldn't be using the cheap and substandard version of this product."

The Boomerang works very well because you are technically agreeing with them, but at the same time, shifting their focus to see how wrong they could be if they looked only from their perspective.

Tipping the Bucket

Earlier, in Step 3 of effectively handling objections, I mentioned that you can dig deeper to bring up more objections. This is, in effect, tipping the bucket of objection so that every possible objection of the prospect will be laid bare. This gives you a clear idea of what exactly needs to be clarified. Usually, all the prospect's objections can be grouped into one or two categories and handled easily.

Here are a few examples of how you can tip the bucket of objections.

"What other reason is stopping you from taking action now?"

"It appears you have more questions. Ask away."

"Aside from this, are there more concerns?"

One of the major reasons why this technique works is that aside from giving you a clear picture of all the reasons they have for not accepting your offer at the moment, it also shows the prospect that you are more concerned with helping them understand better. This is an effective way of building trust in your prospects.

Reframing Objections

This involves reframing objections to mean something entirely from what they have said. You can do this by making the objection sound like a misunderstanding caused by you. For example, you can say, *"I am sorry I must have led you to understand it wrongly. Let me shine more light on that."*

You can also reframe a seemingly insignificant difference as a major difference. For example, you can say, *"Indeed the color is not common. That is what will make you stand out from the crowd."*

Another way to use reframing is to spin the objection around like it is done in the Boomerang. For example, you can say, *"I agree that the house requires some work, but as you said, you want your personal touch to reflect on it, right?"*

Why this method works is simple: you are giving them back what they gave you so it becomes difficult for them to reject their own views.

Pre-empt the Objection

This technique is simple and effective to use and may cut down the time it takes to address objections. It also allows for a free flow of your pitch or presentation. Basically, it means bringing up likely objections even before the prospect thinks of it and addressing it so that it doesn't come up again. The way you do this should make it look like the objection comes from a flawed perspective and then address it rather firmly.

For example:

"Many people will think this is expensive at first, but considering the after-sales service and the payment plan, almost anyone can afford this."

"A few people who hadn't thought it through misjudged it to be too modern for their liking without realizing that technology is advancing."

Pre-empting works because you have effectively shut off the objection before it is raised.

The Conditional Close

This technique works very well during a sale. Basically, when a prospect or client raises an objection you should quickly make a statement that suggest that you will resolve their issues if they too will meet your condition. Your condition could be that they will have to take a second look at your proposal or even signing a deal or making a purchase.

To make this method effective, you should phrase your condition in this form: "if I ... will you..." This is likely to produce better results than phrasing your condition in the form of "Will you... if I..." And here is the reason why this is so. Our brains work very quickly and hearing the words "if I..." gets the mind alerted to something you are offering which makes them want to hear more. But when you start with "Will you..." the brain quickly shifts into resistance because they are already in objection mode and starting by asking them to do something will likely make them not listen to what you are offering.

For example:

"If I can help you figure out a way to get the financial means, will you make the purchase today?"

"If I phone your partner to come over, will you take a look at the details?"

"You said you prefer a blue one. If I can get you one, will you consider buying it now?"

The reason why this technique works so well is that it is built on a principle known as the 'exchange principle' which creates a social agreement that says you are willing to solve a problem for your prospect if they will make a purchase in return.

The Pushback

I have deliberately left this technique for last because I would recommend that you use it cautiously.

The method involves rejecting the objection. In other words, when they object, you should object to their objection. However, you should be mindful not to be antagonistic about it but firm instead.

You can do this by directly telling them when they are wrong or by showing them you are aware they are not being honest. You can also choose to tell them indirectly, and this may likely stop them from raising further objections.

For example, you could say:

"That, sir, is incorrect. This is the cheapest you can actually get for this quality."

"Perhaps you may want to check your figures again?"

"You and I know that you can afford this if you truly want to."

When a prospect knows you are aware of their underhandedness, it makes them want to be on the defensive and rather than bring up more objections, they are likely to want to agree with you to compensate for their insincerity.

When done correctly, directly objecting their objection usually results in shock which is likely to make the prospect accept your point of view.

CHAPTER 3:

HOW TO READ NON-VERBAL CUES

"The most important thing in communication is hearing what isn't said."(Peter F. Drucker, 1909 - 2005, Author and Management Consultant)

Take a good look at your body. It is covered by a layer of skin that allows you to feel your environment. All the senses – sight, sound, smell, taste, and touch – are all tailored towards one purpose, which is, to feel, to perceive your environment. Your environment is made up of other people and everything you can perceive using your senses.

We are designed to relate to our environment and the people in it. In other to effectively relate to people, there is a need for communication – and not just any type of communication, but effective communication. This is where our senses come to play. Apparently, when we discuss communication, many people think of sound and its corresponding organ – the ear - what is required to understand the message being communicated. A good number of other people will add the ability to read and write in other to communicate effectively.

Both are correct. However, communication is not just verbal or written. While the ear is designed to hear verbal communications and the eyes in combination with cognitive abilities can be used in reading written communication, there is another aspect of communication that makes up a large part of human interaction. This is known as nonverbal cues or body language. They are often subtle but they can reveal a lot of information that is not being spoken verbally.

In order to effectively analyze people, you must develop the necessary skills to read nonverbal cues. The reason for this is simple: humans are good at masking their true feelings behind verbal communication. But not a lot of humans know how to mask their nonverbal communication. Therefore, sound knowledge of how to identify these cues will give you an edge in relating to people on a deeper level than they are purposely allowing to reveal. Do note, however, that the art of reading body language is not 100% accurate and are not the same for everybody all of the time. There are a lot of indices that may not make it true for a particular individual like their culture or their natural habits and reactions. These notwithstanding, these common body languages or nonverbal cues are true for many people a lot of the times.

Without wasting much time, let us delve straight into learning how to read cues from different parts of the body.

READING DIFFERENT PARTS OF THE BODY

Head Movements

One of the easiest body languages to read is head movements. However, for someone who is completely ignorant of how to read this glaring nonverbal cue, can hardly explain what head movements are.

Picture a salesman, for example, trying to convince a potential buyer with his sales pitch. The would-be buyer is nodding hurriedly and the salesman continues trying to convince him. The salesman can't read the body language of his disinterested customer and continues wasting his time talking.

Here's another scenario involving the same salesman. He's trying to sell his product to another potential customer. As he gives his usual sales pitch about his product, the would-be customer slightly tilts his head backward, but the ignorant salesman makes no effort to clarify his statements. Obviously, he cannot read the suspicion in his potential client's body language.

Here are the most common head movements and their meanings.

- Quick successive nods are nonverbal cues that say "that's enough, next!" If the salesman in our first example knew that, he wouldn't have continued wasting his time pushing a rope – that is an effort in futility and will get him nowhere.

- A slow nod is a sign of interest in whatever that is being said or communicated. So is tilting the head sideways. This is what you should be looking out for when you are presenting a business idea. If you can get your boss or departmental head to slowly nod his or her head as you are talking, or tilt their head sideways, then your point is hitting the spot.

- During a conversation, if the person listening tilts their head backward it could mean uncertainty or suspicion. If you notice that, it is your cue to clarify your points. The salesman in our second example would have cashed in on this knowledge to clarify his statements. When you notice your listener's head begin to tilt backward, address your last point again or ask questions to know if they need clarifications. Say things like "would you like me to shed more light on that last point?" or something to that effect.

- During meetings, when someone starts to scratch their jaw or their neck, often they are clearly not in agreement with what is currently being said. If you are presiding over the meeting you may want to give them the chance to air their views.

- When in a meeting and you are in doubt who the head or the major stakeholder is, simply watch in whose direction most of the heads turn. The decision-maker gets the most attention while the less-significant persons get less attention.

Reading the Face

The face is one part of the body that most people tend to control in order not to reveal their true feelings. However, you can still read almost imperceptible messages from the face if you study the face carefully. So, if obvious facial expressions like frowns, raised eyebrows, jaw drops, etc, are hidden, you can still read the face by noticing the following:

- A warm smile on the face indicates happiness. In a conversation, it means the person enjoys your company or what you are saying. You will know a genuine smile by the way it lights up the entire face.

- A fake smile indicates that the person smiling wants to show approval even though they do not necessarily enjoy what is being said. You will know a fake smile from looking at the side of the giver's eyes. There will be no crinkles on the sides of the eyes.

- When a person - a subordinate in your office, for example, tells you something about someone or a prevailing situation in the workplace and repeatedly touches their lips with their fingers, that is a sign that they are either lying or not presenting the whole truth.

The Window called the Eyes

Because of the importance of nonverbal cues of the eyes, I have devoted the whole of Chapter 7 to discuss it. However, I'll briefly mention some quick ways you can tell what this window to the soul is telling you.

- Avoiding eye contact during a conversation such as when a shrewd business person is trying to push you into hurriedly making a deal is an indication that they are hiding something.

- Eyes looking down may indicate shame, guilt, or submissiveness. When an honest employee is guilty of something, they are most likely to keep their gaze downwards.

- When you are talking to someone, a colleague for example, and they are shooting quick glances at the door, it indicates they really want to leave your presence.

Hand Movements and Gestures

If you intend to build rapport with colleagues or your boss, or even with customers, you need to get your hand out of your pockets.

- Hands in the pocket could mean the person is being defensive, lacks confidence, and can also mean the person is lying.

- In a meeting or a group setting, when someone keeps pointing to another person unconsciously while they speak, it shows they share some form of affinity with that person. You can cash in on that if you are seeking to get more people to support your opinion in the workplace – getting the support of one of the pair is likely to guarantee the support or vote of the other.

- When talking with someone and they hold an object between you and them, it is their way of saying they want to block you out. In such cases, do not bother trying to sell them anything (an idea or a product). Your work is to get them to trust you first.

- Having palms facing up while talking is a sign of honesty. Such persons are communicating their genuine thoughts. However, if you are a boss, you should realize that honesty, even though a good trait, cannot be the only yardstick for basing your decisions. You should know when an honest view may not be a beneficial view.

Are They in Your Space?

- When someone sits or stands very close to you, their body language is saying they like being around you. If you are selling something (a product or an idea) to them, it is likely that they will buy it or make some form of commitment.

- When you lean in, sit closer, and stand near someone and they pull away, that is a sign that they don't share a mutual connection.

The Feet Don't Hide It

Many people put in a lot of effort into hiding their facial expressions and other forms of body language, but they forget to hide the messages coming from the feet. A person's face may hide their true feelings, but the feet don't lie.

- Notice the direction where the feet of the person you are talking with is facing. That is where they most likely want to go. So if you are presenting a business idea to someone and their feet are facing the door, you should probably round up your presentation.

- Feet pointing towards you is an indication that the person is interested in you or what it is you are saying. Seize the chance to drive home your strong points before they get bored and begin to point their feet away from you.

- Locked ankles are a dead giveaway! If you observe this, especially during a one-on-one meeting with an employee, this has nervousness or apprehension written all over it. They may not want a particular co-worker or anyone else to walk in during the meeting. It may also be that they are nervous about an unfavorable outcome of the meeting.

Watch the Arms

Where a person places their arms speaks volumes.

- Hands akimbo (hands on the hips and elbows turned outward) indicate authority, power, or dominance. This also applies to hands placed on a table while standing especially in a business meeting.

- Hands crossed over the chest usually means defensiveness or disagreement. If you are talking with your employees or subordinates for example, and notice this body language, someone is trying to tell you that they disagree with what you are saying.

- When someone has their hands crossed over their chest with a warm smile on their face, it usually indicates self-confidence.

Body Mirroring

Performing similar body movements and speech pattern as someone else is called mirroring. Here's an example of a natural form of mirroring. When you look at a person yawning, it is likely that you will also yawn.

- When someone mirrors your movements, they are likely into you. Gently change your sitting or standing posture and wait a few seconds to see if they will mirror you.

- If you are a woman and you want to build rapport with another woman, mirroring her exact outfit may kill any chances of doing business with you. Women generally don't appreciate mirroring their outfit.

- Men, on the other hand, see dressing alike as a chance to become good friends. As a matter of fact, that friendship may become a life-long friendship that can culminate into a business partnership.

- Do not mirror negative signals. If you do, chances are the other person will not want to associate with you even though you were mirroring them.

CHAPTER 4:

THE DIFFERENT PERSONALITY TYPES

"And those who were seen dancing were thought to be insane by those who could not hear the music." (Friedrich Nietzsche, 1844 – 1900, Philosopher)

Personality type is a rather broad subject and depending on whom you talk to or what source you are consulting, you can get a varied number of personality types. Nevertheless, for the purpose of this book, we shall limit our focus to the four basic personality types and how their traits drive business decisions either in the capacity of a business owner or an employee.

Understanding that each individual in a business setting is driven or motivated according to their personality type will help you to relate to them from that understanding. It is a lack of such understanding that causes conflict and misunderstanding in a workplace. To accurately analyze the people in a business setting or in the workplace, you need to understand what drives them.

Several names have been advanced for the four basic personality types but their description remains the same. Let us now take a look at the four basic types and what drives their business focus.

THE DOMINANT PERSONALITY TYPE

Also called the choleric personality type, the dominant personality type describes a person who is always objective, focused, and hardworking. They are goal or result-oriented, always looking forward to accomplishing the task at hand and jumping onto the next task. They are natural leaders; therefore, they have no qualms taking the lead.

A business owner with a dominant personality type is purpose-driven. He or she does not care so much how a result is arrived at – their major focus is simply on the result. They keep the big picture of the company or organization in their line of focus and hardly get distracted with petty stuff. They handle relationships with employees in a matter-of-fact or straightforward manner. Their leadership style is driven by a high level of energy. They do not usually tolerate excuses for nonperformance. Their leadership style involves the use of force or their personality.

An employee who has a dominant personality type is always an ambitious worker. They go the extra mile to make sure they outperform their previous performance or the performance of other employees. They are the ladder climbers in a cooperate setting. They have their eyes set on the next available position that will advance their career. They believe they are qualified to handle whatever task is thrown at them no matter the difficulty level, and they are very resourceful.

Working with a Dominant Personality Type

In other to effectively work with someone who is a choleric or a dominant personality type, you need to understand that they take assignments or tasks very seriously. This is why they tend to get really upset if people underperform or do not do exactly what they are required to do. If you work with a boss who has a dominant personality, be sure that you are always on your "A" game and be ready to take on a great amount of delegated tasks. To win their respect, you must appear prepared and very sure of yourself. If they sense any uncertainty in you, you will lose out with them. They like to work with winners or people who have a can-do attitude.

Dominant personality type leaders are quick decision makers. If you work with one, ensure that you provide them with adequate information for them to reach prompt decisions. Getting them to function as better leaders should be your target if you want to be in their good books.

If you want to make a choleric leader attend a function, make them see that all the leaders will also attend.

An employee with the dominant personality type will make a good unit or departmental head. Coordination comes easy for such an employee. Keep them engaged by always delegating tasks to them. To get the best out of them, motivate them by offering them temporal positions of leadership.

THE EXPRESSIVE PERSONALITY TYPE

The expressive personality type is also known as sanguine. They are extroverted and that makes them naturally suited for tasks that involve talking to people and even strangers. In other words, they are natural salespeople.

They are full of high energy and very optimistic. They are not afraid of competing in business and are very open to challenges.

As business owners, they are good motivators and they relate well with their employees. A business relationship for a boss with an expressive personality type is a lot more personal and long-lasting. They tend to make their employees feel great about taking on any challenge. An expressive leader leads by their inborn ability to be endearing.

An employee with this personality trait will make a good marketing professional. They are good at training others in their area of expertise because of their ability to be expressive.

Working with an Expressive Personality Type

A sanguine is driven by their desire to have fun. This tendency for fun usually makes them less organized. If you have an employee with this personality type, they will perform better with tasks that involve socializing or are people-oriented over tasks that require a high level of organizational skill. So, be sure to leave them out of the critical thinking tasks and engage them in areas like marketing or sales. They can use their ability to be charming and likable to lead to more sales and close more deals.

Telling an expressive personality type that an event will be fun is more than likely to get them excited to be at the event. They make excellent MCs at events too because they are not usually inhibited in social gatherings.

THE INTROVERT PERSONALITY TYPE

The introvert personality type is often referred to as the melancholic – these are people who are overly concerned with minute details. They are very analytical and thorough. They are hardly driven by whim when making decisions; their decisions are well thought-out and very calculated. They tend to avoid rash making business decisions by all means. They would rather delay a decision until they get the facts right than to hurry into wrong decisions. Rationality is far more important to them than jumping into decision-making. They are always driven by the voice of reason. However, their desire for a lot of detail tends to keep them stuck in analysis paralysis. And they are most often viewed by others as being very pessimistic or even sluggish thinkers.

A leader who has this personality type will not tolerate employees who bend the rules even if they produce results in the long run. Being morally upright and following due process is a vital character trait for this type of boss. These types of leaders are known to lead by their focus on detailed procedures and company policies.

An employee with an introvert personality type needs a lot of precise instructions. You should spell out exactly what you want to be done and how you want it to be done.

Working with an Introvert Personality Type

A business owner with the introvert or melancholic personality type needs to be kept abreast of all the nitty-gritty of the task at hand. They are interested in all the details that inform a decision.

These types of leaders tend to micromanage others. For you to convince a boss who has this personality type, you must provide ample information in your presentations or pitches. Leave no stone unturned when presenting them with any new business idea.

An employee with this personality type needs to know that their actions are in keeping with the rules of the organization. So, do not forget to compliment them on their rightness and their ability to look at things from several points of view. This is a great way to motivate an introvert personality type. However, if you are delegating a task that requires a relatively quick decision based on scanty details, you should never consider delegating such task to an introvert personality. They simply cannot work with scanty details; neither can they afford to be rushed into making quick decisions. A boss who does not understand this will always have a misunderstanding with such employees.

If you are looking for an employee that will enforce company rules and regulations, you should consider choosing one who has an introvert personality type. They will ensure every other employee in your organization know and keep to the rules.

To get an introverted person to attend a function, make them see that all the information they need will be presented at the function.

THE RELATIONAL PERSONALITY TYPE

The relational or phlegmatic personality type combines a little bit of both the expressive and introvert personality types. Because they are highly relational, they work best in groups and always look out for the interest of others. They are outwardly expressive but do not want to be rushed into decisions just like the introverts. They need time to consider the impact of their decisions on others. However, unlike the introverts, their focus is not too much on keeping to rules and regulations. They may, in fact, go to the extent of sacrificing their own interests to protect those of others.

A business owner with the relational personality type does his or her best to avoid conflict among their team. They are easy going and protect the interest of their workers to the best of their ability. They tend to take the welfare of their workforce very seriously. They are often perceived by their employees as leaders rather than bosses. These types lead best by forming alliances.

An employee with this type of personality flows well with a group. They are good team players who will hardly verbalize their frustrations so as not to create conflict in a team.

Working with a Relational Personality Type

To get a leader with the relational personality type to agree to any business policy, you will have to convince them that it serves the interests of all involved. Other people's opinions are of great importance to them, so when you present a business idea to them, you should ensure that you level the playing field so that the interest of all involved will be properly protected.

If you are looking for an employee that will be a good follower, seek out a relational personality type. Putting them in charge of a team or a unit may not bring out the best in them. At best, they will try to please everyone and in turn fail to meet the company's target.

HOW TO EFFECTIVELY MANAGE DIFFERENT PERSONALITIES IN A BUSINESS SETTING

Briefly, let us take a look at five steps to effectively manage these different personality types in a business setting. This section is designed for those who manage other employees.

Step One – Determine their Type

Obviously, the first step in effectively managing employees of different personality types is to determine what personality types they fall into. Are they thinkers or feelers? While thinkers make their decisions largely from facts and logic, feelers depend largely on relationships rather than objectivity. Observing how each employee handles disagreements and conflicts will give you a clue as to whether they are thinkers or feelers. We shall take a deeper look at this in the next chapter. When you have determined their personality types, you can then adjust your management style as it relates to each individual. For feelers, try to be sensitive while dealing with them. And for thinkers, focus more on facts and logic.

Step Two – Establish a Relationship

Some employees can be difficult both to management and colleagues. However, if you take the time to identify their personality types, it will become easier to build trust and a long-lasting relationship with them. This will eventually translate into strong loyalty and definitely increase work output.

Step Three – Raise the Bar

If you are looking for more productivity, you need to raise the bar for your employees. Standardized work may become too boring especially for employees who detest working under strict supervision. Raising the bar and allowing creativity to come to fore will push them to bring out their best. Key into their personality and use it for the greater good of your organization.

Step Four – Determine their Preferences

Check to see what best suits each personality work preference and tailor your developmental programs to follow those preferences. For example, some work better with regular or instant feedback instead of an annual review. Some may prefer a strict set of rules within which they will operate, while others may prefer the freedom and flexibility to think out of the box.

Step Five – Don't Take It Personally

Realize that not every employee likes the idea of a hierarchy. Many of them may not be particular about you as a person; it is just in their trait to be reluctant about taking orders. Keep this in mind and don't take things too personally. As a leader who has devoted the time to read, identify, and analyze your employees' personality types, you are more equipped to win their trust and that should account for some positive change in their attitude towards being led.

CHAPTER 5:

ADVANCED HUMAN PSYCHOLOGY

"Once you understand yourself, you can stop fighting your natural tendencies and plan for them instead." (Anne Bogel, Reader, Writer, and Podcaster)

In this chapter, we shall quickly focus on how to determine a person's personality type by digging a little deeper into the psychology of the individual. This is a necessary step if you want to establish any useful relationship with others both in a professional or social setting.

HOW TO READ AND DETERMINE PEOPLE'S PERSONALITY TYPE

Carl G. Jung, a famous psychologist, popularized the idea of personality types. Using his model, humans are generally categorized into two broad dimensions, which can be further represented by two opposites, namely:

1. Sensing (S) as against Intuition (N)

2. Thinking (T) as against Feeling (F)

A combination of these results in the four basic personality types denoted as ST (Sensing and Thinking types), NT (Intuition and Thinking types), SF (Sensing and Feeling types), and NF (Intuition and Feeling types).

Note: Intuition is denoted with an 'N' instead of an 'I', this is because another trait which we shall consider later is denoted by an 'I'.

Determining the Sensing (S) and Intuition (N) Types

You can use the following descriptions below to determine if a person falls into the Sensing or Intuition category.

A person who is a Sensing (S) type is usually:

- Very practical

- Depends on specific details such as facts and figures to make decisions

- Focused on the present or current problem and challenge at hand

A person who is an Intuition (N) type is usually:

- Highly inspirational and has good insights

- Depends on trends, theories, and insights for decision making

- Focused and concerned about the future

Determining the Thinking (T) and Feeling (F) Types

You can use the following descriptions below to determine if a person falls into the Thinking or Feeling category.

A person who is a Thinking (T) type is usually:

- Very rational, controlled by reason

- Depends on objective approach and logical analysis to make decisions and solve problems

- Cold, objective, and impersonal

A person who is a Feeling (F) type is usually:

- Very emotional, controlled by feelings

- Depends on values such as good and bad, and instinct to make decisions and solve problems

- Warm, sympathetic, and supportive of others

COMBINING THE TWO DIMENSIONS

When you have identified the individual characteristics of a person, you can then accurately categorize them as Sensing and Thinking types, Intuition and Thinking types, Sensing and Feeling types, or Intuition and Feeling types.

Note that a person may not display the full characteristics associated with their type. However, to accurately place them, you should look at which category best describes them to a large extent.

EXTROVERSION AND INTROVERSION

There is another dichotomy between the dimensions earlier mentioned. This is Extroversion (E) and the Introversion (I). When you further add this layer of categorization, the result will be a more nuanced version of the personality types.

Stated in simple terms, extroversion is interest and involvement with things and people outside of the self. An extroverted person finds his or her motivation from the outside world. Typically, an extroverted person will maintain contact with people regardless of whether their jobs require it or not. They enjoy participating in activities and conversations with others.

On the other hand, introversion means to be self-absorbed and take little or no interest in other people and the world around. An introverted person finds his or her motivation from their inner world. Even if their jobs require having several contacts with other people, an introverted person will rather not make such contact. They will prefer to go into solitude and give thought to what they like and their feelings.

Determining the Extroverted (E) Type

Use the following descriptions to determine if a person is an extrovert.

- Their energy, drive, and motivation comes from external sources
- They initiate or respond to events in the outside world
- They enjoy having numerous contacts with people
- They enjoy talking and expressing themselves in groups
- They do not mind interruptions or others getting into their space

Determining the Introverted (I) Type

Use the following descriptions to determine if a person is an introvert.

- Their energy, drive, and motivation comes from within

- They are focused on and think deeply about the inner world

- They prefer to avoid numerous contacts with people unless it is very necessary

- They prefer one-on-one conversation

- They do not like interruptions and like to have their space to themselves.

COMBINING IT ALL

A combination of all the characteristics from the Sensing-Intuition and Thinking-Feeling dimension together with the Extroversion-Introversion dimension will further split the 4 basic personality types into a more nuanced 8 personality types. Hence, our earlier 4 basic personality types will now become:

1. Extroverted, Sensing, and Thinking types (EST)

2. Extroverted, Intuition, and Thinking types (ENT)

3. Extroverted, Sensing, and Feeling types (ESF)

4. Extroverted, Intuition, and Feeling types (ENF)

5. Introverted, Sensing, and Thinking types (IST)

6. Introverted, Intuition, and Thinking types (INT)

7. Introverted, Sensing, and Feeling types (ISF)

8. Introverted, Intuition, and Feeling types (INF)

CHAPTER 6:

READING BASIC BODY LANGUAGE

"What you do speaks so loud that I cannot hear what you say" (Ralph Waldo Emerson, 1803 – 1888, American Essayist)

Body language is nonverbal cues and signals that form part of our communication. Experts opine that it creates a huge part of our day to day communication. The ability to understand and use this body language to your advantage will go a long way in ensuring your success in whatever endeavor you find yourself.

Whether you are trying to close a sale deal, do business, be successful at an interview, are with friends or a lover, the body language of the parties involved speaks volume. Studies show that it forms over 60% of the entire communication process. With this in mind, it is essential to learn how to read body language.

From facial expression, to eye direction, to the shape of the lips and posture, body language has a lot to say about what is going on in someone's mind. This is why body language can help a salesman make many sales and win over a prospect. It can give an interviewer insight into the candidate and help judge what the candidate is saying through his body language.

Being able to pay attention and decode body language effectively can help in the success of your career. To a salesman, for instance, he should be able to decipher clearly what the prospect is saying with the body, the same way he hears the words.

An interviewing panel should also be able to pick clues and information from an applicant's body language. He should be able to pick answers to some questions by carefully analyzing the candidate's body language, even before hearing the candidate speak.

Humans generally hardly pay attention and do not react to body language.

Seeing someone smile, for instance, is an indication that the person is happy and has received you warmly. The right response in this scenario is to return the smile

How to read Non-Verbal Body Language When Doing Business, Making a Sale, or in an Interview

Great salesmen and people in business have honed the act of paying attention and decoding the body language of their prospect. They are able to take advantage of the smallest clue which most people will ignore and can use that to consciously change their tactics to work in their favor.

The best part is that reading body language is not rocket science. It is a skill that you can learn and with practice, become an expert at. This part of the book will analyze critical pointers that you should pay attention to. In whatever sphere of life you are in, it is sure to help you.

The Eyes

Eyes, they say, are the windows to the soul. This is very true as a mere look into the eyes can reveal a lot about someone, like what is in the person's mind. Your candidate's eyes, your prospect's eyes, can reveal a lot of information. This is because man has little control over the pupils. In fact, it is one of the few body parts you cannot control.

Let us consider this. Although, I won't be surprised if you already know it unconsciously.

When trying to close a sale for instance and your prospect is focused on you, this means they are paying attention to you and what you are saying. If they are looking at your goods, it means they are thinking about it.

If while making a sales presentation, for instance, and you have part of your audience checking out your paperwork, they might have a question. When anyone is staring at the door, it might be an indication that they can't wait for the business meeting to be over. A simple way to make things interesting is to let them have the floor. Let them ask questions to voice out their concerns.

Keep in mind that if you have a prospect, there is a big chance they will not look at what is on their mind. It is normal for them to move their eyes around the room a little bit. But all in all, their gaze will return to that very thing that is on their mind.

In a one-on-one meeting, for instance, a prospect staring down at you might be an indication they have something to say since they might not want to intrude. Try and pause for them to air their concerns.

Be sure to remain relaxed and calm during the entire engagement with the client. Try and employ a soft sell approach to help the client feel in control. Have in mind that staring is not so good. It is an indication that your prospects have maintained around 80% eye contact with you, which is considered too high.

Aim for an eye contact of about 60 to 70%

Pupil dilation is an indication that your client is thinking with total focus. This is very helpful and can be a good sign when reading through a contract or a resume. Besides, it has been agreed that when the pupils widen up, the person is happy with what they are learning. Narrowing pupils indicate that they are upset, confused, or have concerns.

When you see that your prospect's pupils suddenly become narrow, ask about their concerns. Or, better still, take that as a cue to focus and expound on the point that triggered this. While being interviewed as well, a candidate can use this information to study the interviewer's reaction to help him gain the upper hand.

Watch for Facial Cues

Humans have an innate ability to use their face to communicate. Even a baby or toddler can smile or frown as an expression of their emotions. And this is one of the first things babies learn to do.

Mind you, there is a wide range of emotions and thoughts humans can express consciously with their face. On the other hand, there are quite a lot that we convey unconsciously as well.

While being interviewed for instance, if your interviewer keeps smiling and nodding, that is a good sign. This also applies to the business setting when closing a deal. If your client or interviewer is doing both or either, you are in for a smooth sail.

In the same way, if either the face or neck reveals any tension, the client or interviewer is unhappy, suspicious, or has concerns. You can see this manifest as a crinkling of the nose, pursing of the lips, etc.

Be sure to encourage your prospect to talk. Your aim should be to address their concern, and without them voicing it out, you cannot do so.

Learn to Decode the Gestures

Bear in mind that if the position of your client or interviewer's arm is considered open, it is an indication that they are receptive to the process. Take note of welcoming gestures that flow naturally with the process. Hence, if your prospect or interviewer is reaching towards you often and uses a lot of hand gestures, it indicates reception and is a good sign. In contrast, watch for folding of arms, a tight grip of the arms or wrists and clenching of a fist. This usually points to an unhappy person.

During the business process, whether business negotiation or interview be sure to pay attention to the hands and arms. They are one of the best ways to reveal emotions. For instance, during a business conversation you are having, the hands of the other person might rest comfortably on the table. If suddenly, during the interaction, they pull their hands under the table, it might indicate that something went wrong.

Bear in mind, someone making sincere disclosure will usually gesticulate or show their hands!

Pay Attention to the Shoulders and Torso

The shoulder and torso are also vital components in decoding nonverbal communication. As a rule, if your clients or customers or interviewers like and agree with you, they will tend to lean toward you or come closer to you. On the other hand, there is a significant tendency for them to create space between both of you if you say something unsettling or they disagree with you.

With the above in mind, people turning their shoulders and torso away from you already are no longer interested in the relationship. This usually signifies disengagement from the person, regardless of what you say. When someone is interested and engaged with you, their torso will face you directly. But, as soon as the feeling of discomfort sets in, they might turn away – literally giving you 'the cold shoulder.' Also, if someone shields their torso with a briefcase, their purse, or a book, they are acting defensive.

All in all, make sure you are paying attention to these clues without making it visible. The fact is we have all read body language one way or the other, even unconsciously. However, be sure to analyze the signals you see and make it work to your favor.

NONVERBAL COMMUNICATION CUES TO IMPROVE BUSINESS SUCCESS

Nonverbal communication has to do with using body language to get what you want. People have used nonverbal communication over the years. The previous section has analyzed how to recognize and decode various body languages to help achieve success in whatever endeavor you on.

This section will focus on making you pass on the right message through your body language. This will set you up for success in whatever field you are in. Trying to close a deal, going for an election manifesto, trying to convince a client to invest in your idea, or going for a job interview, be sure to use these body language techniques to get what you want.

Walk the talk

You do not only have to be in a conversation setting to pass the right message with your body language. Even while walking, be mindful of the way you carry yourself. Walk with your head straight, high and erect. Walk with your chin raised, looking straight ahead.

Learn to walk with strength and confidence. Avoid shuffling along and instead, pick up the pace. Walk fast like you have places to go and people to see. Let your walking style make people perceive you as active, busy, competent, and confident.

Give a Full and Firm handshake

When meeting people, your clients, or an interviewer, for instance, give a full, firm and strong handshake. This is one of the ways people perceive a first impression, which can set you up for success or failure. There are some nonverbal communication clues that are passed along when people shake hands.

For instance, in shaking hands, people can judge your character. Many have associated a firm and robust handshake with the right attitude. Hence, they assume that you come offering excellent service to them.

Weak, half, or indifferent handshakes (or even offering the fingers), on the other hand, don't give a good impression about you. It could pass you off as unconfident.

Make a Good First Impression

You are meeting your client or interviewer for the first time. Be sure to offer your hand and look the person directly in the eye, with a warm smile. Offer a greeting like: "Hello" or "How are you?" This is a vital first impression that you do not want to mess up. It can set the stage for a successful business relationship if done correctly.

Sit Erect, Facing Forward

It is essential to care about our body language in business and formal settings. When having an interview or before a client, for instance, avoid leaning against the back of the chair. Instead, face the interviewer or prospect directly. You do not want to look extraordinarily relaxed and lazy about the interaction. You should sit with your back erect and lean slightly forward. Be alert and present throughout the engagement.

The body language of the person we are interacting with can influence us a lot. You make your client or interviewers interested in what you have to say when you sit straight and lean forward. You get the other party interested in what you have to offer the client, rather than putting up a relaxed posture.

This kind of posture unconsciously passes the message that you are on a mission with an important message to convey. With this, the other party will pay attention to you, as opposed to when you are leaning back and feeling relaxed during the interaction.

Get the Other Party to Open Up

When in a business conversation, interview, or when trying to make a sale, you should aim for the other party to open up. An understanding of nonverbal communication cues will be of great help in getting insight into their state of mind. For instance, you don't need a soothsayer to tell you that if the other party is sitting with either hand folded or legs crossed, it is not a good sign.

A person sitting with a closed hand automatically closes his mind to all you have to say. Folded arms are the body's way of unconsciously blocking out incoming data. An unfolded arm, on the other hand, means precisely the opposite.

On noticing this, you should be getting your target to open up. This is quite simple to do. You can ask questions. If that fails to relax them and their arms are still folded, hand them something physically, like a brochure. With this trick, you can get them to open up more to you and increase their interest in your message.

Employ Positive Body Language

A crossed leg is a nonverbal form of communication that could indicate someone is holding back information. The legs can be crossed at the feet or the ankle. They both pass the same message.

In a business setting, for instance, bear in mind that your client will likely want to mimic your body language. Hence, be sure you make optimum use of this body language to win over your client. Avoid folding your hands and crossing your feet. Your prospect might mimic this, which will affect the purpose of the engagement.

Be sure to nod, smile, pay adequate attention, and sit with your back straight. There is a big chance your audience or client will engage in the same body language.

Imagine how being able to employ these tactics could make you better off in whatever endeavor you find yourself. How beautiful it is when you can close deals with ease by using these tactics. It doesn't come naturally, but with time, practice, and persistence, you can consciously build your nonverbal communication skills and make it work for you.

CHAPTER 7:

THE POWER OF THE HANDSHAKE

"To build your self-image, you need to join the smile, firm handshake and compliment club." (Zig Ziglar, 1926 – 2012, Author, Salesman, and Motivational Speaker)

Remember how we talked about non-verbal cues in Chapter 3? A handshake is one of the very first non-verbal cues that reveal a lot about the personality of a person who we are meeting for the first time. It is body language that announces who you are. The ironic thing about a handshake is that most people are not trained on how to give a proper handshake that conveys strength, confidence, and assurance even though it is a very clue into a person's personality. Think about it, we are trained on how to dress to give a good impression at an interview, we are trained on how to present a speech, how to say what we want to say, and even what to say. But little or no training is given on one of the very first forms of physical contact we make with the people we are trying to impress.

WHY IS A HANDSHAKE SO IMPORTANT?

Going back in history, the handshake was a friendly way to show a stranger that you are not armed and had no weapons. In more recent times, science has shown that "a handshake preceding social interaction enhanced the positive impact of approach and diminished the negative impact of avoidance behavior on the evaluation of social interaction" (Beckman Institute for Advanced Science and Technology, 2012, n.p.).

The world we live in today has evolved far beyond the days when a handshake was seen as a mere greeting to demonstrate friendliness; your handshake speaks volumes about who you are and what should be expected of you. It creates a very lasting first impression about you, especially in the business world. If you are thinking of closing a deal, landing a job, making a good first impression on a client, or getting a subordinate to know you are in charge, then you need to work on perfecting your handshake.

Equally, as someone who wants to successfully analyze people to see if they are worth doing business with, or worth employing, or worth trusting, you must begin to see your hand – your right hand in particular – as an instrument for sizing up or assessing the overall personality of the people with whom you interact.

Another important thing about the handshake is that mastering it puts you in a position where you can easily master your professional image. You can choose what message to pass across by simply changing the type of handshake you deliver for different occasions. And yes, there are handshakes that suit different settings such as business, political, religious, or social settings(you do not want to give a fist bump in a job interview, would you?). There is a time and place for different types of handshakes; knowing and using this gives you an advantage of being easily accepted in different settings.

No matter how well you have prepared for a situation, giving a poor handshake or the wrong type of handshake for any given situation or social setting may be your greatest undoing.

As simple and as brief a handshake is (usually between 3 to 6 seconds), it sets the tone of future dealings with the people you meet in both a business setting or social gathering especially if you are meeting with them for the very first time. In sales, a simple handshake is capable of making or breaking a long sought-after deal. A simple handshake can equally change your entire career positively or negatively.

The point here is simple: a handshake, when properly done, is capable of opening up doors for long lasting business, career, sales, etc, but when done poorly, it can shut the doors of so many promising opportunities.

Additionally, the simple and brief gesture of a handshake can demonstrate respect and it can also be a way to initiate physical contact in such a way that doesn't appear intrusive.

TYPES OF HANDSHAKES AND WHAT THEY SAY ABOUT YOU

There are several types of handshakes and quite a few modifications of them. I shall list a few and briefly show you what they mean. Note that the names I used in referring to these handshakes may differ slightly from the names you may know them by. And as a matter of fact, several names have evolved over time for the same types of handshakes. But it does not matter what you call them. What matters is, knowing how they are done and what they convey about you.

Dead Fish

Also known as the limp fish, this is probably the most awful type of handshake! This type of handshake has no vigor, no squeeze, and no energy at all. It feels as if you are holding a lifeless cold fish in your hands. Do not give this type of handshake unless you want the other person to disconnect from both your hand and anything to do with you. The Dead Fish handshake is obviously a deal-breaker, a career buster, and should be avoided by all means.

This handshake says that the giver has low self-esteem, or is indifferent. It indicates that the giver has a passive or reserved personality. If you give this type of handshake, you are screaming to the receiver at the top of your lungs that you are uninvolved, uncertain, or you are nervous.

Fingertip

Also called the Queen Fingertips, this is when only the fingers are offered during a handshake such as when a queen offers her hand to her subjects, hence the name Queen Fingertips. Many women tend to do this. What this says about your personality is that you prefer to have your personal space either because of insecurity or because you want to keep the other person at arms-length. Unless you are truly royalty or you truly dislike the receiver, you should avoid this type of handshake.

The Pusher

This has the same attitude as the Fingertip except that The Pusher holds hands fully during a handshake but extends the arms so that the receiver does not come close to them. The Pusher handshake says the giver needs their personal space and for you to relate to them you must respect their emotional and physical space.

The Glove

This is commonly referred to as the politician handshake (since they use it a lot). It is a handshake where one hand is used to shake and the other is used to cover the receiver's outstretched hand. This handshake says you are very confident in yourself or you are in a place of authority. It can also be used to express sympathy such as when it is used by ministers. But since it can easily be misunderstood as being overconfident, it is not suitable for professional or business settings.

Bone Crusher

This type of handshake applies an extra squeeze on the receiver's hand, almost crushing it. It signifies an intimidating personality or an emotional bully. If you do not want to come across as someone who is aggressive, then avoid this handshake by all means. Ensure that your grip during handshakes do not become too firm because that could be bad for business.

The Dominator

This is also called the Top-Handed Shake. It is not the usual palm-facing-sideways type of handshake, rather, the giver's palm faces downwards in such that it covers the receiver's hand and stays on top of it. It says that the giver is trying to show dominance and may likely have a superiority complex. If your aim is to prove superiority, this is the type of handshake to use.

The Controller

This type of handshake pulls your hand towards the giver or your hand is literally guided towards a certain direction. This says the giver has a controlling personality. They are more than likely to dominate everything and everyone in their space.

Sweaty Palm

A sweaty palm during a handshake says you are nervous or not confident in yourself; it says you are apprehensive and uncomfortable. If your hands naturally tend to be sweaty, or even if you are truly nervous, you could mask this by discretely wiping your sweaty palms with a paper towel before a handshake. If you are looking to close a deal with an important client, do whatever you can to avoid a sweaty palm during the handshake.

The Proper Handshake

In other to deliver a handshake that will portray you as being open-minded, intelligent, and confident, it is important that you give a proper handshake that conveys the right message. This will be a dry, firm, and palm-to-palm as well as web-to-web handshake. Keep your thumb up and your fingers straight during the handshake. Ensure you put on a smile as you shake the receiver's hand.

HOW TO GIVE A PROPER HANDSHAKE

So, we have talked about why it is important to learn how to give a good handshake and what a handshake tells about your personality. Now, let us learn how to give a proper handshake in five simple steps. These steps can be used for people you are meeting for the first time or for friends and colleagues.

1. Stretch out your right hand with your palms facing sideways and fingers outstretched.

2. Firmly hold the other person's hand without exerting too much pressure.

3. Shake their hand once or twice.

4. Look them in the eye and make sure to smile. It tells them you are completely aware of them and you appreciate their time.

5. Show how verbally confident you are by introducing yourself. You could say, "Hi, my name is..." and you say your name (or whatever line you wish to use. Just remember to keep it short and simple). If you are meeting someone you already know, it goes without saying that you should skip this last step.

When you can effectively combine a good handshake with eye contact, plus verbal confidence, you will make a very good first impression on whomever it is you are meeting. They are not likely to forget you.

Although it may seem tricky to remember how to do this properly the first few times, it is not really difficult to master. As always, practice brings about perfection, so do not fail to practice. Of course, you should not wait until you meet the next stranger or your next client before you practice. Start with your family, friends, colleagues, roommates, etc. I know it may feel awkward trying to introduce yourself to your kid brother with a handshake, but see it as an opportunity to practice not letting the awkwardness show up in your handshake.

And just in case you tried but failed to deliver the perfect handshake to someone you are meeting for the first time, do not beat yourself up. Have some cards up your sleeve like a compliment or a question that can easily distract the receiver of your poor handshake. It is true that you do not get a second chance at making a good first impression, but you still have time to make up for a bad impression.

TIPS TO GIVING A GOOD HANDSHAKE

- Free your hand: Ensure that you have your hand free, especially your right hand as it is most commonly used in handshakes. Do not fill your hand with stuff that you will have to clumsily start moving to the other hand or look for a place to drop when it is time for a handshake. And by all means, do not put your hands in your pockets as they will make you appear unapproachable unless of course, that is your aim.

- Know when to initiate a handshake: This could be a bit tricky. Initiating a handshake can be seen as being in charge or being proactive, or it may be read as being rude in some settings. Make sure you understand what the particular situation or culture calls for before you initiate a handshake.

- Feel the hand, read them: The reason handshakes say much about a person is because they are somewhat personal. You get to have personal (physical) contact with another person. It is a perfect opportunity to read them. So, make sure your palms are not cupped or your fingers bent. Wrap your fingers around the other person's hand and in that brief moment feel what their hand is telling you without needing them to necessarily say a word.

- Use your elbows: Let the movement of your hand come from your elbows, not your wrist. With a firm grip on the other person's hand and thumbs locked, shake their hand for about 2 to 3 times before releasing.

- Convey your message with your eyes: A touch of hands without a meeting of the eyes is an incomplete handshake. The eyes, they say, are the window to the soul. There are lots of unspoken words conveyed through eye-to-eye contact. Ensure your eyes meet the other person's eyes to convey your passion, respect, power, or self-confidence.

- Unexpected handshakes: There may be times when you didn't expect it, but someone had just stretched their hand as they walked towards you and you automatically felt inclined to shake their hand, placing them in charge of the handshake. At such times, you can turn the tables on them by giving them the glove handshake. This will slow down their momentum and put you in charge of the handshake.

- Watch the direction of your palms: There are times when your palms should face upwards, and there are times they should be sideways. For example, when you are sitting and the other person is standing, you can choose to outstretch your hand with palms facing upwards. It is an excellent move to use when you are not too sure if the other person will reciprocate your gesture. But use this sparingly as it gives the other person the chance to be in charge of the handshake. On the other hand, when you are both standing, ensure that your outstretched hand faces sideways and give a firm grip when shaking hands.

- Be mindful of your body language: Your posture during a handshake matters also. If you are standing during the handshake, ensure that you lean in just a little bit with both feet firmly planted and make sure you face them. In the event that the handshake is taking longer than usual, you can step back a bit to make them break the hold. If you are seated, ensure that your back is erect as you stretch your hands for the handshake. Do not bend over or bow except if the setting calls for it (such as greeting royalties).

- Informal handshakes: Handshakes such as the fist bump or any type of secret handshake may not be quite suitable for persons with whom you are not very familiar. For buddies and colleagues, it may be appropriate especially if you are aiming for extra effect. Using a fist bump or giving a dap in a formal setting or for complete strangers may cause them to perceive you in a light that is not good for your professional image.

- Avoid these: Do not pat the other person on the shoulder unless you are their superior (as in boss, employer, or minister) or you are in a position to convey care or sympathy (perhaps to show support or empathy for a loss). Also, give the other person room to shake your hand. Do not hold their hand in a clasp and yank it before releasing. The other person will have no option but to just follow your hand movements without enjoying the brief contact.

CHAPTER 8:

USING EYE SIGNALS THE RIGHT WAY

"I like getting to the meat of things. You can't get it in a five-minute interview. I like to hone a person. I like to make eye contact." (Larry King, 1933, Entertainer, TV & Radio Host)

To effectively read, analyze, and manage people, you must first stop seeing them as annoyances or obstacles. The eyes of the people you meet on a daily basis hold a wide range of emotion that tells a story. There is something about the eyes that says a lot about a person's thoughts in the present moment. The eyes may not readily tell you about a person's overall personality, but it sure gives you clear clues about what they are most likely thinking at that moment. Even infants can read people's thoughts by looking into their eyes and responding appropriately. They can pick up subtle messages from the eyes of parents and adults.

This chapter will show you how to read people from their eyes by outlining the different eye movements and what they mean. We shall also learn how to take advantage of this knowledge to make the right eye contact in different situations.

THINGS TO REMEMBER
WHEN INITIATING EYE CONTACT

- Eye contact leads to more eye contact: People generally may not want to initiate eye contact because they feel the other person may not welcome it. Initiate the move; they may look away at first but try again and they will follow suit. If you have tried twice or thrice and they keep avoiding contact, it is best to let it be.

- Don't be creepy: Eye contact, when done correctly, can pass on the appropriate message. However, when it is not welcomed and you continue to stare, it becomes unnerving. Remember, even if the other person is not looking directly at you, they can sense when you have your eyes focused on them as if they are prey.

- Switch from one eye to the other: Try to place your focus on one eye for a bit and then gently move to the other eye. Be careful not to dart from one eye to the other as that can be distracting. When you move smoothly from one eye to the other, it gives the other person a sense that you are paying attention to them. Avoid staring at the bridge of the other person's nose. It can be misread as trying to be manipulative.

- Don't be too obvious: Avoid locking eyes for the entire period of a conversation or interaction. It is okay to look away for a bit.

- Don't look down when you break gaze: Always remember to look sideways when you break your gaze. Looking down will send a message to the other person that you are submissive. It may also mean shame or low status.

- Practice with familiar people first: You will be surprised to find that you do not even maintain eye contact with the people closest to you such as your family members. Practice with family and friends first, then you can move on to colleagues, and then to strangers.

COMMON EYE MOVEMENTS
AND THEIR MEANINGS

Raised Eyebrows

When the eyebrows are raised, it draws attention to the general look on the face. A raised eyebrow is generally interpreted as wanting to communicate better. Use your eyebrows to send quick non-verbal messages such as wanting to be understood or when you want to create emphasis. You can experiment this in front of a mirror. Look into a mirror and say "do you understand?" without raising your eyebrow. Now repeat the same thing in front of the mirror but this time raise your eyebrow. You will notice that with your eyebrows raised, it adds emphasis to what you are saying.

Darting Eyes

When someone can't seem to keep their eyes still while in your presence, it means they are uncomfortable or they feel insecure. Their eyes are telling you that they would prefer to not talk with you at that moment. If you must portray a confident presence, do not let your eyes dart even in the presence of the most intimidating client, boss, bully, or the opposite sex.

Squinting and Eye-Blocking

When someone squints at you it is very likely that they do not like what you are saying. Squinting often means the other person is suspicious or does not believe what you are saying. When someone squints at you, directly address their doubts and make your point clear.

When someone blocks or covers their eyes, it means they do not like something they are seeing or hearing at that moment. When someone blinks a lot or rubs their eyes a lot, it is also considered eye-blocking. The act of blocking the eye is actually a natural reaction to repulsion. This can be observed in children who are born blind when they cover their blind eyes when they hear some unpleasant news.

Gazing

A very personal way to communicate with the eyes is by gazing. It conveys intimacy or disagreement depending on the situation where it is used. Gazing into the eyes of a beautiful woman or a handsome man usually tells them you like them. On the other hand, gazing or staring straight into your boss' eyes for a few seconds longer than usual conveys disagreement or opposition.

If you want to convey power or authority, use the power gaze to stare down the other person. Maintain a steady look within the triangle of both eyes and their forehead.

If you aim to show comfort or support, use the social gaze to stare at the other person making sure your gaze goes within the triangle of both eyes and their mouth.

And if you intend to create a feeling of intimacy in the other person, use the intimate gaze. Let your eye movement go from their eyes to their mouth and down to the body. Your eyes are saying loud and clear that you are having intimate thoughts about them. If someone is staring at you in this manner, you know exactly what they mean.

Glancing Sideways

This could be a bit tricky, so you need to pay extra attention in other to accurately read what it means. When someone glances sideways with their brows furrowed, it shows that they are uncertain or that they require additional information. It can also mean that they feel critical or suspicious.

Another sideways glance that can easily be confused with the above is when someone glances sideways with their eyebrows up. This is an indication of interest, and in some cases, it could mean intimacy is intended.

The difference between the two is the furrowed brow and the raised eyebrows. Once you get that slight difference you will be able to tell the two apart.

Looking Down the Nose

When you look down your nose at someone, you are sending a strong message that says you feel superior to them. Use this when you want to remind an unruly subordinate that you are in charge.

Peering Eyes Over Glasses

When someone peers at you from over the lenses of their glasses, it gives the impression that they are intimidating. If you are the one doing the peering, you could use one finger to slightly pull down your glasses for more effect. In a business setting, a woman who wears glasses is perceived to be more impressive.

LYING VERSUS REMEMBERING EYE MOVEMENTS

When someone is telling a lie, you can detect it from the direction of their eyes while they are talking. Generally, a person who is lying will look up and then look to their right. It is an eye movement that indicates that they are, at that moment, using their imagination or are simply lying.

On the other hand, when a person looks up and then looks to their left, it typically indicates that they are, at that moment, using their memory. They are trying to recall or remember something.

Nevertheless, ensure that you understand the orientation of the person, whether they are right- or left-handed. This is because the direction of the eye movement is reversed for a left-handed person.

SUBTLE SEXUAL EYE CLUES FROM THE OPPOSITE SEX

You cannot completely rule out attraction even in a business setting. After all, every business is built around human beings who by nature are social beings. Here are some subtle eye messages that tell you someone in a business setting is attracted to you. You can use this knowledge as leverage but be careful to not take undue advantage of the opposite sex. I'll limit these clues to only 3 since this section is not focused on eye clues in a courtship or relationship.

The Helpless Look

When a female colleague or client plucks her eyebrows higher up her forehead, it gives them a look of helplessness. This helpless look works like magic on men because the man's brain is cued to secrete hormones to defend or protect a woman when he sees this look.

As a woman, you can use this to your advantage to get your way with men (closing deals, getting a second chance, etc). As a man, you can use this to your advantage and know that the female is simply trying to play over your intelligence.

The Come Hither Look

This look is almost always communicated from a woman to a man. It is simple and may pass unnoticed. It involves simply looking up and to the sides.

If you are a man who knows this look, you can cash in on it and play along to get what you want. As a woman, this eye movement gives you deniability. It is not too obviously flirty but it surely passes the same subtle message especially when done with an evasive smile.

The Orgasmic Look

When a woman looks at you with a raised eyebrow and lowers her eyelids, it gives her an orgasmic look. This is a bold move from a daring woman. As a man, tread carefully. Unless she is your intimate partner, it is obvious she's trying to manipulate you into a business decision that may not favor you (or your company) in the long run. A woman who is a go-getter and who will stop at nothing (morally right or wrong) will usually use this eye movement to be extra persuasive on her male counterparts.

A Word of Caution

Do bear in mind that many business settings do not encourage intimate relationships between colleagues. And in some cases, it may not be healthy to have an intimate relationship with clients. Ensure that you do not violate any code of conduct when using this knowledge.

USING EYE CONTACT IN DIFFERENT SETTINGS

Eye Contact in Sales and Business Settings

When you are trying to close a deal or sell something, it is important to make eye contact with clients as this will help to build rapport. Be on the lookout for when they say something or ask a question and look into your eyes. It is their way of saying "what's your honest view about this?" Seize the moment to address their concerns making sure you hold their gaze long enough to establish trust.

There are usually a handful of people in a room when you are making a pitch. Remember to make eye contact not just with the head of the group, but also with the deputies and other subordinates. It is like you are taking everyone into consideration and not just the head.

For job interviews, ensure that you maintain healthy eye contact with the interviewer. Avoiding eye contact during job interviews is a telltale sign of insecurity or lack of confidence. Seldom will any company be interested in hiring such a person.

When you are in a situation where you have to give feedback (critical or positive) to a subordinate, avoid sitting in a face-to-face position. It is a feedback session, not an interrogation session. Arrange the sitting position in such a way that the other person sits about 45-degrees across from you. This position makes it effortless to shift your gaze from the subordinate's eyes to your paperwork.

Eye Contact When Giving a Speech

Making eye contact when you give a speech puts you forward as one who is confident, competent, and trustworthy. Maintaining eye contact with your audience creates a deeper connection and allows your message to be easily welcomed.

Try to make actual eye contact even if your audience is very large. Do not follow the advice that says look above their heads – you can't fool anyone with that. You definitely can't make eye contact with everyone in a large audience, but you certainly can make eye contact with a few individuals. And do not pan your head from left to right as if spraying them with some invisible laser. Neither should you be darting your head back and forth between your notes and your audience. The first order of speech-giving you should handle is to memorize your speech or make a note of the major points so that you will only have to glance once in long while at the few major points.

Eye Contact for Complete Strangers

If you must learn how to handle all sorts of people, you should make the effort to learn how to make eye contact with complete strangers – even those you randomly meet on the street. Firstly, make sure that you do not appear intimidating or threatening. Keep a neutral facial expression with a soft gaze. Secondly, initiate eye contact only when the person is about 4 paces from you. And finally, briefly look into their eyes, perhaps for long enough to quickly notice their eye color. In the event that they look back at you, offer a brief smile.

Eye Contact to Show Power

Making eye contact when you are listening to someone speak, regardless of who has a higher status, is a sign of being charismatic. But when you really want to display power or authority, it is best to make eye contact when you speak and less eye contact when you listen. Making more eye contact when you speak puts you in a position of being submissive.

You can also hide your eyes to show power. Using dark shades, mirror shades, or sunglasses can effectively mask feedback from your eyes. The one-way eye communication puts you in charge because you can see their eyes and the message it conveys, but they can't see yours. Have you noticed that police officers in dark shades appear intimidating, or people who don't take of their sunglasses when indoors tend to get on others' nerves?

Another way to show power is to stare the other person down. Maintaining a fixed stare in a non-romantic setting shows dominance. Looking away shows submission. Staring someone down is a way of sending a strong domineering message to their psyche. A classic example is seen among wrestlers or boxers.

CHAPTER 9:

THE QUICKEST WAY TO BUILD RAPPORT

"Rapport is the ability to enter someone else's world, to make him feel that you understand him, that you have a strong bond." (Tony Robbins, 1960, Entrepreneur, Author, and Motivational Speaker)

The truth is, you are surrounded by people who may share the same interest as you, but if you do not know how to connect with them on a deeper level, you might be missing out on a wealth of resources that these people can provide. This is why I have devoted this chapter to show you the quickest way to develop strong connections with the people you do business with.

Rapport is the friendly link, relationship, or connection between people based on mutual trust, likeness, and an understanding of each other's concerns. In order to improve your chances of building stronger bonds between you and your business partners, colleagues, clients, prospects, and customers you will need to learn proven techniques to build a strong rapport with them.

If you follow what is outlined in this chapter, you will know how to deliberately make the important people in your life feel strong positive thoughts about you. You and them will have mutual respect for each other and hold each other in high regard. You will both share a certain level of coordination which gives the feeling of being in harmony or in sync with each other. In a nutshell, following what is outlined in this chapter will help you build rapport faster with the people who matter to you especially in your professional life.

Now, let us dive straight into the techniques for building quick rapport. First, we shall discuss the two main ingredients that can quickly improve rapport building, and then we shall also go through six quick tips required for building rapport.

MASTER THESE TO QUICKLY BUILD RAPPORT

Have you ever met someone for the first time and feel they are easy to be with? The reason is simple: something in them reflects part of you. They were consciously or unconsciously mirroring your gestures, posture, seating position, the tone of your voice, expressions, and even your body angle. It didn't take long before you began to feel that there was something about the person that you like. This happens because they were mirroring your body language and your speech patterns. Mastering these two ingredients quickens the pace with which rapports are built.

You can use body mirroring and speech patterns to influence people to be freer with you. For example, a boss may want to create a relaxed atmosphere with an anxious employee by intentionally mirroring the body language of the subordinate. Copying the employee's gestures and posture may make the employee loosen up and feel freer with the boss.

On the other hand, a subordinate can also mirror the body language of his or her boss to show support or agreement with the boss's opinion.

This is a subtle but powerful way to influence others. They will literally "see" that you understand them completely and make them feel comfortable around you.

If you learn how and when to mirror the body language and speech pattern of someone that you like, it will definitely pay off big time. Be careful not to be too obvious though because that will simply annoy and put them off.

Now, here are the steps you need to learn in other to master the art and science of mirroring.

Feel Your Connection

The very first step you need to take is to feel your connection. If you are not feeling connected to a person, it is very likely that they are not feeling the connection either.

To feel your connection do all you can to make the other person your center of attention at least for the period of your interaction or conversation. Deliberately place yourself directly in their line of view (if possible, in front of them). Make eye contact frequently, nod to show you are paying attention, and gradually shift from merely pretending to really feel truly connected to them.

Mimic the Pace

Mimicking the way a person speaks, that is, their speech pattern, is a good way to create instant connection too. Observe if the other person talks slowly, fast, loudly, or calmly and try to follow suit. If you have the same accent, that is a bonus too! Mirroring speech pattern is less obvious that body movements, but it has the same powerful effect as body language mirroring.

Look for the Punctuator

Everyone has a punctuator they frequently use to drive home their point. It usually is a body movement such as a hand gesture or a facial movement like the raising of eyebrows. If you do pay close attention to someone, even if you are meeting them for the very first time, you will be able to identify their favorite punctuator. To show that you are paying attention to them, subtly use their favorite punctuator when showing that you agree with them. You are most likely to make an instant connection with them at this point. For example, a person who snaps his fingers to drive home his main point will connect easily with you if you snap your fingers when saying something like, "ah! I see your point." As a matter of fact, there are some punctuators you use without saying a single word and still make an instant connection.

Test

The final step is to test the connection to see if it is not a fluke. You can skip this step though because it is completely optional. And if you choose to follow this step, once or twice is enough to test it. Doing a repeated test is capable of ruining everything.

Here's how to test your connection. Simply make an obvious body movement that is not related to the conversation at hand and observe if the action is mirrored by the other person. For example, you can scratch an imaginary itch, interlace your fingers, cross your legs if you are sitting, or tilt your head and watch what happens. If they mirror your movement, you know that you have established a quick connection with them.

6 TIPS TO REMEMBER

Prepare for Impact

Everyone has an opinion about someone they are meeting for the first time. Whether we are aware of it or not, we all have a way of sizing someone up or judging someone we are meeting for the first time. It is a human thing. And that is why first impressions matter a lot.

The very first step to building rapport with people is to create a positive impression, especially on the first meeting. Knowing that you will be judged (consciously or unconsciously), it is in your best interest to be at your very best (or close) when you are meeting people or someone for the first time.

From dressing to cleanliness, and to your general mood or energy that you radiate – let people perceive life and vigor from you. It is normal for people to be attracted to those who radiate liveliness and shrink from those who emit doom and gloom. In other words, putting on a long face, a frown, or a disappointed demeanor will only serve to push people away from you. Remember, it is difficult to get a second chance to make a good first impression.

Every single person you meet in a professional setting is a potential source of opportunity. Therefore, prepare your mind and your appearance for impact – for positive first impact. You never know which connection will take your career to the next level.

Remember the Essentials

Having taken the first step to prepare for positive impact, you should always keep in mind the essentials or basics of human interactions we have discussed so far in previous chapters.

When you are meeting with humans like you, give a good handshake coupled with steady eye contact and let your smile be the icing on the cake. No matter how well-dressed you are or how clean you appear, if your first handshake is poor and you can't look the person you are meeting in the eye, you have just tanked your first impression!

Another essential thing to keep in mind is paying attention. Do not just hear what is said; listen to what is said. And to show you are present and paying attention to what the person is saying, give a nod every once in a while. You do not want to overdo it or nod vigorously. That will be considered trying too hard and will send the wrong signal. Remember that your interactions must not be non-stop conversations. Give room for short silence breaks to gather your thoughts before resuming the conversation.

It is not enough to know how to read body language. What you should also be concerned about when meeting people is what is your own body language saying? What does your body posture say about you? Are you all over the place? Are you trying too hard to make your acquaintance? Or do you appear calm and collected? Does your posture say you are self-confident without being arrogant? Are you relaxed or tensed? Are you wearing a confident smile or a sheepish smile?

Equally, it is important that you are clear and succinct when you speak. Do not bombard people unnecessarily with whatever knowledge you presume you have. Moderation in all you do is very vital in building rapport, especially with new people. You do not want to be perceived as someone who is desperate or someone who is a showoff. Remember to be transparent also. Transparency has a way of drawing like-minded people to you. It is an instant turn-on for a lot of people, just as dishonesty is an instant turn-off for many people.

In a nutshell, you should keep your verbal and nonverbal communication at top gear if you intend to build a strong rapport with people.

Emphasize Similarities or Commonalities

In its basic meaning, rapport simply refers to a feeling of similarity or commonality. When you find and emphasize the similarities you share with others, it has a way of making you feel you've known each other for a very time even if you just met the same day. A common example is you may like the same sports as them or share the same hobby. When you talk about the things you like and are passionate about, you tend to let down defenses or barriers and allow the other person to come into your life.

Note that just sharing your passion for football, for example, may not necessarily translate into liking everything about the other person. To build a strong rapport, you need to keep looking for more commonalities and similarities. The more things you can find and emphasize, the deeper the level of connection.

Don't Fake it

One quality that will endear you to people is being yourself. Being honest and genuine makes easily people develop trust in you. Do have it in mind that you are unique. Therefore, it is pointless to want to be another person. What you are looking for are people who have the same interests as you. If you hide your true self behind a mask, how will the people who share the same interests as you recognize and be drawn to you?

In other to build a strong rapport with others, you must keep in mind that negative behaviors such as cheating, lying, or backstabbing are a no-no. These behaviors are capable of destroying everything you have built. Avoid them like the plague.

Read Body Language

It is important to perfect your verbal communication first and then ensure that your nonverbal cues synchronize with what your words are saying. If you put in the effort to make your words and your body language agree, then it will be easy for you to recognize nonverbal cues in others too.

Humans communicate on several levels – words are just one level. The body speaks on a deeper level than mere words. Connecting with people on a deeper level requires a deeper understanding of their nonverbal communication. Reading body language tells you who truly shares your interest, who is faking, who is trying too hard, and who is hiding something.

Throughout this book, I have dropped several clues and tips on how to effectively read body language. Take the time to study them in other to improve your body language reading skills and connect deeply with people.

Empathize

There is a very good reason why people associate easily with people who are emphatic. It is because most people have an underlying need to be understood. If you can leverage this, then you can build very strong rapport in the shortest possible time.

You see, we all view the world using different lenses. Our lenses are shaped by our beliefs, fears, environment, and so many other indices. This is why it is easy to judge others as wrong because they do not see things from the same vantage point as we do. Their words and actions are easily termed inappropriate to many except the few who know how to empathize.

That is to say, if you can place yourself in someone else's shoes and view the world from their unique perspective, you will most certainly not judge them harshly. The ability to look at things from other's perspectives is difficult for most people, and as a result, only the few who have developed this ability can truly connect on a deeper level with others.

If you empathize, you will not take things personally. You will understand that people's views about you are simply that – their view. It does not reflect who you truly are. Flip the coin and the same applies to others. Your personal views about others do not reflect their true persons. They are just your views.

This may seem to contradict the purpose of reading people in order to form an opinion about them. Well, there is no contraction whatsoever. Rather, when you perfect your skills on reading people, you will not only accurately create an informed opinion about them, it will also help you see their point of view and therefore connect with them on a deeper level. Remember, you are not learning to analyze people because you want to judge them. What you are doing is to understand them in other to better relate to them.

The Bottom Line

It is indeed simple to build long-lasting rapport if you know how. Nevertheless, do not see building rapport as a daunting task. You can do it. After all, we are all social beings except that some of us have allowed ourselves the freedom to express that social part of us more freely than others. If you really want to tap into the abundant resources that are deposited in the people around you, you should allow for a stronger connection with those with whom you have identified as having similar views as you.

Remember, you are not taking undue advantage of the people around you by building rapport with them. You are only developing a robust social circle by using these proven techniques for the betterment of everyone involved.

CHAPTER 10:

ADVANCED FORMS OF
BODY LANGUAGE READING

"What you do speaks so loud that I cannot hear what you say" (Ralph Waldo Emerson, 1803 – 1882, Philosopher)

In Chapter 3, we discussed common body language and their possible meanings. In this chapter, we shall take that knowledge a step further by looking at some nonverbal cues that are more evasive. If you can identify these cues you stand the chance of greatly improving your evaluation and subsequently arriving at better decisions.

Keep in mind that I shall be discussing this with particular reference to a professional setting. However, the principles hold true for social settings or any other particular scenario you find yourself in. Do note, however, that the context within which any particular nonverbal cue is expressed will ultimately determine the meanings that signal holds. It is also worthy to note that you should not base your evaluation on one single nonverbal expression. Combine two or more body languages in other to get a relatively accurate reading of someone's hidden or nonverbal intentions.

The following are some of the more subtle body languages and their possible meanings.

UNCROSSING ARMS AND LEGS

When you are presenting an idea or pitching a product, notice if your audience is crossing their arms or legs. If they are, take a short break from your presentation and make them uncross their arms and legs. You can do this by directly asking them, or if it is not appropriate to ask them directly, you could try changing their position or doing something that will make them uncross their arms and legs.

So, what's in uncrossing of the arms and legs? When arms or legs are uncrossed it improves memory. Your audience is unconsciously blocking you out with crossed arms and legs – it is a defense body language. Uncrossing them will allow more memory retention of what you are listening to.

GLANCING AT THE TIME

When someone takes a quick look at the clock or their wristwatch they are passing a very clear message that says I need to be somewhere else right now. Unless you are observant, you may not catch this quick glance.

When you are pitching a sale to your prospect or making a presentation to a board of executives, it is imperative to pay close attention to them and notice if they are unconsciously telling you to round up your presentation.

You can also use this body language to signal someone in a meeting that they are taking longer than necessary especially if the person is your subordinate or employee. Doing this when someone superior has the floor can be seen as being very rude. Avoid it by all means.

THE CHIN JUT AND BATTLE STANCE

These two body languages are usually rare in a professional setting unless there is serious pressure to meet a deadline or some other form of pressure.

The chin jut usually indicates anger, while the battle stance which has a person placing both hands on their hips with their feet widely planted means rage. While this may not resort to a physical fight because of the professional or business setting, it usually is followed by a barrage of verbal exchanges of hurtful words.

When you notice a person going into the battle stance or having a chin jut, it is your cue to quickly change the subject of discussion or completely avoid them for that moment. Take a break to allow strained nerves to calm down. If you must keep talking about the same issue that is causing the tension, be sure to direct the conversation into something reassuring or pacifying.

SMILING

This may seem like common body language, and indeed it is. However, it does not always mean what people think it means.

Smiling has been commonly identified as the body language for friendliness. Nevertheless, when someone smiles too frequently, it does not indicate that they are very friendly or welcoming. On the contrary, they are unconsciously saying they are weak or submissive.

As an employer, if you notice an employee always putting on a smile when you are talking or when they are in your presence, they are telling you they are fully loyal and submissive to you. These are the types of employees that will go the extra mile for you.

As an employee, you can use smiling to be in favor of your boss. But if you do not want to be seen as weak, you should drastically cut down your frequency of smiling.

LEGS AND FEET

As earlier mentioned in Chapter 3, it is difficult for most people to hide their true feelings from showing up in their legs and feet. But I am not just talking about the feet pointing towards you or the door which may be interpreted as meaning the person has an interest in you or is secretly wishing to leave the meeting or conversation. The feet convey more than that and unless you know how to read advanced body language, you may miss out completely on the other messages that the legs and feet convey.

When an employee begins to shuffle their legs especially when in a seated position or wrap their feet around a piece of furniture or around each other it is a sign that they are under a lot of tension. If it is an interrogation, they probably are trying to cover up something. Increased feet and leg movements signify increased stress and anxiety.

When you have to interrogate someone, it is good practice to make them sit in a position that gives you a clear view of their entire body. This way, you can observe their feet and leg movements more clearly.

LOW TONE

Speaking in low tone conveys authority. This is the perfect voice tone for a boss or a leader. If you are in a room with several people and want to know who the authority figure is, listen to their tone. This does not necessarily mean the person with the deepest voice is the boss. Remember that a woman can also be the boss and yet can have the lowest tone of voice.

When you want to show that you are in charge, drop voice tone to its lowest. But many people do not know the tactics to keep their tone down. So when they speak, their tone takes away the authority in their words even if they occupy positions of authority.

Here's a quick tip to keep your voice tone low.

Let your voice slow down to its optimal pitch by placing your lips together and humming or making the "um hum, um hum" sound repeatedly for a couple of seconds. When you eventually speak up, your voice tone will significantly drop. For females, ensure that your voice drops when you end your sentences. If you keep your pitch high at the end of your sentences it will sound as if you are seeking approval even when you are giving a direct order. Or you will sound like someone asking a question. Try practicing and getting used to the authoritative arc, which means, when stating your opinion or making sentences, your voice should begin on one note, rise in pitch as you are speaking, and finally drop down at the end of your statement.

FACE-TO-FACE

In a meeting or presentation, sitting face-to-face with the speaker unconsciously tells them they have your undivided attention. Even if your sitting position will not allow for a direct face-to-face, you can turn your head and torso towards them. Checking your phone, multitasking, or looking to see how others are reacting may not encourage the speaker. This also applies in a one-on-one situation. So, if you want the other person to speak up and let their sincere opinions out, assume the face-to-face position.

THE POWER POSE

Standing with legs and arms open is the power pose. It indicates self-confidence. If you are doubtful or unsure and you need to boost your confidence especially when addressing your superiors, assume the power pose for a few minutes and your confidence level will rise.

This has to do with the hormone testosterone which is associated with dominance and power. The power pose stimulates the release of testosterone both in males and females.

If you find yourself training employees on how to give a presentation that will influence their audience, teach them the power pose.

CHAPTER 11:

THE EASIEST WAY TO BUILD CHARISMA

"How can you have charisma? Be more concerned about making others feel good about themselves than you are making them feel good about you." (Author, Dan Reiland)

Are you running for mayor of your town?

Are you a salesman hoping to close some deals?

Are you a pastor who wants to connect more with your congregation?

Are you an entrepreneur seeking to attract investors?

Do you want to increase your circle of friends?

Are you a parent trying to strengthen the relationship with your child?

Charisma is one potent tool for success that can help in whatever sphere of life we find ourselves in. Charisma is that quality that makes people like you, which will also attract people to you naturally and makes people want to listen to you. It is an essential trait for leaders who want to get on the right side of their followers.

Charisma might seem like a hard and mysterious quality to develop – something some are born with. The good news, however, is that you can build charisma. With dedication, practice, and commitment to the three main arms of building charisma, you can transform yourself into a person that commands grace and is liked by everyone.

In learning how to build character, this book will focus on three significant arms of developing charisma – presence, power, and warmth. A strict commitment to these three can be the beginning of a healthy and happy transformation in your life.

FIRST CHARISMA COMPONENT: PRESENCE

Whenever you are discussing something with someone, and you feel you don't have their total attention, I bet you feel quite annoyed. A lot of people are guilty of this. People hardly engage with other people during the interaction.

When you look at this in the light of developing charisma, it means making yourself captivating to other people. No, this is not about tooting your own horn; it is about making the other person feel good about themselves. In other words, a brief moment of interaction makes the other party feel good about themselves and leaves them feeling better than you met them.

To create this captivating feeling, you have got to focus your emotional and mental energy on the other party. People love being recognized and acknowledged; it is an inherent human character.

Conveying presence is simple yet could be difficult for some people to achieve; here are some helpful tips to developing it.

Bring Yourself into the Conversation

In other words, practice mindfulness. We have difficulty being in the present because we are not mindful. While we might be interacting with someone, our mind is a mile away, engaged in other things. A little trick to help with this is direct your attention on body sensations, most often the breath. It is not about paying your attention to your breath but using it as a trigger to bring you back into the moment.

Be Physically Comfortable

Be sure you are comfortable on the seat and in your clothing. Paying attention will be hard if all that occupies your mind is how uncomfortable you feel. In this regard, choose a comfortable posture. If you are engaging people in your home, set the thermostat to a comfortable temperature.

Maintain Eye Contact While Talking

It has been established that people who make eye contact convey warmth, sincerity, confidence, dominance, honesty, and emotional stability. Besides the fact that eye contact makes you appealing, it also helps you have quality interaction. With eye contact, you build intimacy, with the other party feeling warm, confident, and connected to you. Be careful, however, not to make the other party uncomfortable with too much eye contact.

A Nod to Affirm you are Listening

You can also use head signals to illustrate your presence, besides eye contact. Body language, especially nodding, helps as well. You, however, have to be careful again with nodding as excessive nodding could be interpreted as trying too hard to please the other person. This, without a doubt, will work against you. Bear in mind however that to nod appropriately, you have to be listening to the person.

Ask Clarifying Questions

A simple way to let the other person know that you are with them throughout the conversation is to ask clarifying questions. This, however, should be when the person is done talking. For instance, questions like "when you referred to_____, what were you talking about?

You could also rephrase part of what the person said and add, "Am I getting you right?"

That is just a part of the equation. After presence comes power and warmth, let us get on with the second element of developing Charisma – Power!

SECOND CHARISMA COMPONENT: POWER

When we mean charismatic people are powerful, it doesn't mean they wield massive power; neither are they rulers of empires. It is often said that great power lies in humility.

Power:

"...means being perceived as able to affect the world around us, whether through influence on or authority over others, large amounts of money, expertise, intelligence, sheer physical strength, or high social status." according to Cabana.

Increasing your charismatic power comes with practice. It is not something you develop overnight. Here are some ways to boost your charismatic power:

Improve Your Confidence

To exhume power, you have to feel powerful from within. For it is when this happens that you can radiate this energy to others around. Self-assurance and confidence help draw people to you, and to be confident, you have to develop your mastery. Whatever field you are, be an expert, a person of knowledge, a resourceful person who knows what he is up to. For it is when you attain mastery in your field that you will feel confident which will reflect in the way you carry yourself.

Know Something about Everything

Okay, maybe something about everything is a bit of an overstatement, but I think you get the point. The idea is to be vast in many subjects, know a little about many things. Bear in mind; you cannot affect the world around you without intelligence. Besides, the more conversation you can comfortably add and contribute to, the smarter you appear to people.

The simplest way to build this is to read whenever you can!

Be Smart with How You Dress

One of the most influential power cues is clothing. This is why military men and law enforcement agencies are adorned in unique attire as it demonstrates authority. With a high-status outfit, you can influence others. Bear in mind that this is not entirely about being seen as powerful, but also feeling good about yourself, something you can get from dressing appropriately.

Be sure to take steps every day to dress better. It is not about burning a hole in your pocket to get the latest designer outfits. We are talking about reasonable upgrades to show you are on top of your game.

Assume Power Poses

Some poses are believed to convey power. The arm akimbo, for instance, is a familiar and favorite power pose. This is why we see many superheroes in this position.

You can also lean back in your chair and have your hands interlocked behind your head.

You could convey power in a meeting by standing and leaning forward with your hands on the table before you.

Another power pose is lifting your hands in the air before you. Be smart about when you want to use this pose though, so you do not come off as strange.

The beautiful thing about the power pose is that besides making others see you as powerful, you also feel manly as well. This, according to research, can help increase testosterone level and decrease cortisol. With this, you feel confident and less stressed, which helps in your quest to develop charisma.

Take Control of Your Environment

Familiarity with our environment makes us feel less anxious and at ease. With this comes a sense of control which boosts our confidence. This explains the reasons why firms tend to argue strongly concerning the venue of a negotiation. They do this before negations commences. The goal is simple; each party wants a home advantage.

Speak Less and Speak Slowly

Being powerful is not about physical space alone. Instead, you have got to engage in conversation as well. It is not about dominating the discourse, mind you. Powerful people understand the value of making few words heard, for it is in this that their communication will be valued. Hence, powerful people don't talk as much as others, and so when they do, people listen.

Powerful people are not bothered by the "awkward" silence; rather, they love it. They space out their conversation with silence. Typically, people are usually desperate to fill the silent gap. Powerful people know that the other party will likely give out vital information, a useful advantage during those periods of anxious chatter. This explains why job interviewers, interrogators, etc., resort to silent treatment to bring out the person's vulnerability. Remember in the chapter about lying, the first point under signs of lying is that a liar is never comfortable with silence, hence, he keeps blabbing in a bid to fill the silence with claims.

On a final note about developing charisma, I will explore the last piece of the puzzle – warmth. For it is only when you can successfully harness the three arms that you will develop charisma.

THIRD CHARISMA COMPONENT: WARMTH

With warmth, people perceive you as caring, gracious, empathetic, and above all, approachable. They are at ease, comfortable, and can be themselves in your presence. Warmth has to deal with the human need to be loved, taken care of, and to be understood. This is something that has been instilled into man right from childhood.

Warmth is a mother packing an umbrella in a child's bag before they go to school. Warmth is a father pecking a child's forehead as he lifts them up after coming back from school.

Although we grow up and fly out of the nest, deep down, we still crave for that feeling of being accepted and being cared for!

Warmth is essential and works perfectly in sync with the other two elements before it can help build charisma. If you have power without warmth, people will see you as arrogant. And if you have warmth without power, people see you as weak and an attention seeker.

In developing warmth, try and adopt the following points.

Practice Gratitude

With gratitude comes joy of heart. Besides, people who are fond of practicing daily gratitude are happier than others who do not. There are many ways you can practice gratitude. Every day, for instance, make a list of things you are grateful for. As you develop this, you can put your problem in perspective, and you are more relaxed which radiates to people around you.

Prioritize Face-to-Face Relationships

A face-to-face connection and interaction with other people is what triggers empathy in the brain. This explains the research that says college students these days are less emphatic, compared to their counterparts 30 years ago. This is because they prefer communicating and relating with people online rather than through physical interaction. When we don't connect physically, the possibility of being indifferent and exhuming an evil motive is there. Hence, reduce the time you spend on the phone chatting and in front of your computer screen and interact with people offline.

Be Genuinely Interested in Others

To develop warmth, you have to show that you are interested in getting to know the other party. Ask clarifying questions that reveal more of their personality. With this, you understand them and know what gets them going. From everyone you interact with, you can learn something about the person and life in general.

Give a Firm Handshake

Touch is also essential in generating warmth in others. This is not about flirting and invading other's personal space. The handshake is a good chance to establish skin-to-skin contact, make it firm, warm, and full of life.

Alongside the firm handshake, offer a smile. This will keep the other party relaxed and connected with you.

Keep Details, Anniversaries, and Dates in Mind

I have come to notice that when people remember my birthday, especially people that are not close to me, it makes me feel special. And I bet other people think this way as well. This is not about littering someone's Facebook wall with birthday greetings. You want to stand out from the crowd.

Send a card, make a call, or craft an email. See this as an opportunity to ask about their wellbeing as well. In addition to that, keeping details in mind is very important.

Give Thoughtful Gifts

I am not asking you to burn a hole in your pocket to get someone a gift. It does not have to be something big. I am talking about things that let people know you are paying attention to them. Your wife has often come back from work soaked in the rain. Getting her an umbrella is very thoughtful. You can imagine how glad she will be when you mention that you hate seeing her drenched every time.

Smile, it Costs You Nothing

With a smile, you not only feel warmth but also convey warmth to others. It is one of the easiest ways to express warmth.

Smiling is so powerful that studies have shown that it can make you happy instantly even when you don't feel satisfied. Go ahead and grin, it will pave the way for a warm mindset.

Besides making you happy, smiles make you confident, approachable, and more attractive to others. Also, research revealed that people who smile often are more attractive than others who do not. One thing anthropologists and psychologists have come to agree on is that smiling is a tool which signifies to others that we come in peace or we have good intentions.

I can go on and on about how smiling helps you and contributes to your quest to build charisma. It will cost you nothing. Be sure to train yourself to offer a smile to everyone you come in contact with.

Relax Your Posture

Depending on the circumstance, an erect posture might make you appear cold and stiff in some situations, even though it reveals power and confidence. Hence, if you are trying to create warmth, have a relaxed posture.

Don't stick your chest out and throw your shoulders back. Instead, assume a natural and comfortable position with your back, shoulders, and chest. You want to look approachable, not like a dictator.

Mirror their Body language

There has been a study that affirms that when you copy how someone talks, and also mirror their body language, you build trust with them and they also find you attractive. According to psychologists, mirroring another's body language triggers limbic resonance between the two parties, creating strong feelings between them.

Be careful, however, not to make it too apparent or you appear as if you are mocking them. If they talk slowly, slow your voice down as well; if they lean back in their chair, lean just a little bit back as well. Be sure to wait a few seconds before mimicking their position.

There are times when mirroring a body language could backfire. You don't want to mirror an angry person's tone or body language. This will inevitably escalate the whole issue.

CONCLUSION: BUILDING CHARISMA

I am pretty sure if you have followed this book thus far, you will agree that charisma is not a quality for a certain group of people. Instead, it is something you can build with time, patience, and practice.

The tools provided above are infallible in helping you build charisma. It, however, does not come on a silver platter as you have to practice until the habits become part of you. In time, you will be able to create a balance between the three components which will transform you to a loveable person whom everyone wants to be around.

Charisma as a trait can be used for both good and bad, being a neutral trait. However, be sure to use yours to increase your circle of friends, draw people to you, make people like you, increase your sales, and strengthen your relationships with people altogether. Be sure to engage in worthy causes both professionally and socially; charisma will open doors for you that won't for those without charisma.

CHAPTER 12:

DEALING WITH OBJECTIONS

"To build a long-term, successful enterprise, when you don't close a sale, open a relationship." (Patricia Fripp, Author, Speaker, and Sales Presentation Trainer)

In this final chapter, we shall be discussing how to know when people will object or reject what you are proposing or offering. The best way to know this is by learning how to read rejection body language that only experts can read.

When presenting a business idea, making someone an offer, or pitching a sale, your job is not just to make an excellent presentation. Your job also includes listening to what your audience is not saying. In other words, you are not just talking with your mouth and hearing with your ears; you are also "hearing" with your eyes and your perception, the messages their body language is sending. The aim of this chapter is not just to get people to accept your ideas or products, but to connect better with them and help them see your point of view.

SIGNS OF OBJECTION

Below are examples of body language that indicate objection or rejection. Watch out for them and tackle them effectively even before your audience verbalizes their objections. It will be as if you are in their heads, reading and analyzing their minds.

Hands and Arms

Sign language is based entirely on hands and finger movements. This means the hands can say a lot more than many people realize. In a meeting or a presentation, watch out for the following hands and arm signals that tell you objection is brewing, and then take appropriate steps to address the yet-to-be verbalized objection.

- Your prospect begins to play with objects like a pen: They are telling you they are bored. This could also mean they are annoyed. In both cases, give them the chance to become part of the conversation by asking them questions that will require them to share their thoughts about what you are offering.

- Your client is drumming his or her fingers: This is one of the clearest signs of impatience. Your client may not be interested in all the details you are sharing with them or simply doesn't have the time for lengthy presentations. When you notice this body language, skip the nitty-gritty and hit the main points.

- Their hands are crossed or their body and hands are turned away from you: These people are telling you they do not like or are not interested in what you are saying. Bring up another subject or find another way of offering the same idea or product, if not, end the interaction and save both of you some time and energy.

- They are pointing fingers at you or your product: This hand movement says they are trying to intimidate you. Calmly addressing your client's concerns or questions may take care of the situation.

- They are leaning on one arm or resting on an armrest: That person (your employee, boss, or client) wishes to leave the meeting. A great way to quickly tackle this is to give them room to air their views. Note, however, that this body language may not be very accurate; therefore, you should not always draw your conclusions by isolating this sign alone.

Feet and Legs

If you cannot figure out exactly what a person's facial expression means, look at their feet. People hardly consciously control their foot and leg language, and if they are in agreement with you, the feet will easily reveal it.

- When a client is wiggling his or her feet or legs, that's a sign that they are bored. Perhaps you have been doing all the talking and it is time to involve them in some of the talking.

- If your potential buyer, client, or employer is tapping their feet, it's likely that they feel they've got the upper hand, an edge, or advantage in a negotiation. This may not seem like the body language of objection, but it sure tells you that you are not on the winning side.

Eyes

The pupil is one of the very few parts of the body that can't really be controlled. When someone is about to reject or object to your offer or proposal, it cannot be hidden from their eyes.

- When a prospect's pupil narrows, it is more than likely that they have serious concerns about what you are presenting. In such a case, you should slow down with your pitch and ask if they need clarifications about something you have said.

- When someone is staring you down while you are talking, it is obvious they have some concerns about what you are saying. If you are selling an idea or product, you may want to stop and ask them if they have questions about your offer. If it is your boss, you should politely ask if they have some concerns about your ideas. And if it is an employee or a subordinate, you can ask them (if appropriate) to air their views.

- When a prospect's eyes keep returning to a particular area/object, your paperwork, for example, they may be worried about having to fill out all the information required. You should ask if they have some concerns about it, and assuage their worries.

- When someone's eyes keep glancing at the door while you are talking, they are unconsciously telling you they want to leave. If you are not done with your pitch or presentation, cash in on the clue and re-engage them by letting them be part of the conversation. However, if you are done with your pitch and there is obviously nothing further to say, wrap up and let them leave. This will save all concerned some valuable time.

Others

Watch out for the followings also:

- Pursing of the lips: This indicates that they are not telling you something they think about what you are presenting. Perhaps they are being polite not to offend or hurt your feelings but they definitely are not going to agree with you. When you see this body language, give them a chance to air their opinion. They may not be forthcoming at first, but with a little bit of persuasion, they will tell you what the objection is.

- Crinkle of the nose: This indicates mild disagreement. When you see this, the prospect has an objection but they are unsure if they are right or wrong about it. The objection is still taking form in their minds so they may want to hear more before they decide to voice out. Cash in on this mild disagreement gesture and nip it in the bud before it develops into a full-blown objection. Ask them to tell you what their concerns are no matter how slight or trivial the concern is.

- Tension on the neck or unconscious scratching of the back of the neck: This indicates serious doubt. When you notice this body language from a superior for example, take a quick pause and ask if something you have said in your presentation is out of order or amiss. They may help you get your facts straight.

All of the above are signs that your client, employee, boss, or customer is about to object or reject what you are proposing or offering. To increase the chances of them listening to you till the end of your pitch or presentation, you should pause and address their concerns or give them the floor so that they can also be part of the talk or share their concerns.

CHAPTER 13:

HOW TO WIN ARGUMENTS

"That's the beauty of argument, if you argue correctly, you're never wrong." (Christopher Buckley, 1952, American writer)

In the good old days, philosophers would persuade people using short, direct questions aimed at exploiting ignorance. On spotting weaknesses, philosophers would direct their disciples as they wish, based on their reasoning. Being able to argue was a gift!

These days, we argue at work, with our spouse, friends, etc. We argue outside the courtroom, online, etc. Arguments are usually undesirable because people do not like losing or backing down. However, winning an argument can be a display of mental rigidity.

BUILDING THE FOUNDATION FOR WINNING

Arguments are used to persuade an individual or an audience about a topic. It involves appealing to reason with a touch of passion and emotion. An argument is better with a single individual because it helps tailor your points.

In establishing how to win an argument, I will explore the ancient trick employed by Aristotle. Aristotle used three modes of appeal: pathos, logos, and ethos. These three appeals to reason is a means to explore inner doubt in the opponent. It leverages on a particular way of forming opinions.

Pathos has to do with appeal to emotions. When arguing, you aim to get your opponent to appeal to the point you are making. A salesperson trying to convince a company to invest in a Fire extinguisher Ball could appeal to the emotion of the safety officer of the company. Hence, he could say things like: "Investing in this Fire extinguisher Ball will improve your competency in the company."

Logos is an appeal to logic. Still, on the illustration above, he could recall facts that help his cases. For instance, Fire extinguisher Ball removes the extra expenses of servicing a fire extinguisher. This leads to saving money for the company. You have got to know who you are arguing with to be able to use this approach. You need to see if they need facts or simple assurance. However, for Logos to yield, you need the points yourself.

Now here is where ethos comes in. This has to do with character and the arguer's credentials. For you to win an argument, your point should be legitimate enough to convince people. In other words, you should establish yourself as an authority in the field. Let people see that you are knowledgeable.

HOW TO WIN AN ARGUMENT

The above only sets the stage for the argument. Psychology has many branches which can help steer an argument in your favor. The human brain reasons well with logic, emotions, patterns, and numbers.

During the argument, emotion is a powerful weapon. Although exploiting emotions like panic and fear is purely diabolic or manipulative, feelings like vigilance are good. These emotions align with the human brain, and if you can recognize them in your opponent, you have the upper hand already.

Making eye contact during an argument, for instance, might not help in persuasion. This, however, opposes what many cultures passed down about being assertive – that eye contact and a firm handshake help establish dominance.

When trying to win an argument, however, you want cooperation and not dominance.

Eye contact is considered intimate and reserved for certain situations. Animals, for instance, will only make eye contact when they want to establish dominance. This explains why a dog will look at each other eye to eye before fighting.

You also cannot afford to show weakness. Your aim should be finding common ground with your opponent. Quite a lot of studies have established that the mirroring technique is a subtle way to build rapport. Hence you can mimic your opponent's body language and speech patterns. More of this in the next section.

Understanding and Mastering the Art of Arguments

Dale Carnegie in his book - How to Win Friends and Influence People – advised that the best way to get the best out of an argument is to avoid it. He suggested strict avoidance of arguments as if they are the plague. This is, however, a wrong view of the argument, an incorrect interpretation of the point of argument.

The only situation when I would recommend the advice above is if the argument also comes with a physical fight Many people see arguments as a competition where one person stands with the trophy and others get knocked out in the process.

Having this mindset about arguments undermines reason. If you view an argument as a competition, then cheating will help you win. This is when you interrupt people, convince them with horrible arguments, and call their views ridiculous, stupid, or crazy. You can even go as far as making a jest of their ignorance, how little knowledge they have. While this trick might help you win, it cannot help you understand their point.

There is, however, a better way to win an argument. Imagine you believe that new mums should get up to six months paid leave, and I do not. This makes you see me as selfish and heartless; I might consider you as irresponsible. We have both failed to understand each others' view hence we don't respect one another. As a result of this, there is no ground for compromise, no meeting point. However, suppose you buttress your assertion with the end that: a six month paid leave gives new mum enough time to bond with their little one. I might counter you by saying that employers will lose out if they paid for six months of work. This gives both of us the chance to understand our positions and acknowledge our shared values.

In reality, an argument doesn't go this smooth. Failure to listen to our opponent or trying to understand their reasoning deprive us the opportunity of learning from them. A constructive and reasonable conversation where both parties express their opinion becomes hard when neither side gives any points to defend their position.

Failure to understand the point of an argument (to appreciate one another and find common ground) is why people tend to avoid it.

Also, many arguments are plain bad. People assume they give good reasons without really presenting anything. Hence, when people say things like: You are wrong because you are ignorant, there is no basis for the conclusion reached. No one benefits from jumping to such erroneous conclusions. Instead, the idea is to discuss and exchange ideas amicably. Analyze issues from premises to end. To do this successfully, you need the skill of proper and unbiased evaluation – how to differentiate a good argument from a bad one. Evaluation majorly involves sieving out bad arguments and admitting reasonable arguments. There is also palace for humility in an argument as you need to be able to accept your weakness and acknowledge that the other party's reasons outshine yours. While you do not have to let go of your conviction, your knowledge about the issue and your opponent would have increased.

Without a doubt, arguments are not easy. This is why the next section will explore the dos and don'ts of an argument. Your brilliant ideas are worthless if you cannot tactically and logically communicate it to the other party. Before I continue, I will discuss some dos and don'ts alongside some clever tactics to twist any argument in your favor.

Dos:

1. Stay Calm: No matter what, try and separate emotion from the argument. Don't lose your temper or get sentimental. If you do, you lose.

2. Use Facts to Buttress Your Points: The salesman in the example above had facts. Hence, persuading the safety officer that fire extinguisher balls were better than fire extinguishers was pretty easy. Be sure to arm yourself with facts, statistics, etc. these make up the perfect arsenal that can help support your case.

3. Ask Questions: Mastering the act of asking a question in an argument can disorganize your opponent. They will scramble for answers, leaving them disoriented. Simple questions like where/what is your support for that claim? Employ the power of hypothetical questions as well. For instance, questions like: How will everyone be better off using this technique?

4. Employ the Power of Logic: Employ the power of ideas following each other. Use this to build your case and see how it can undermine your opponent

5. Appeal to Higher Values: You can tap into the power of emotions by appealing to worthy causes or motives that are hard to disagree with.

6. Listen Attentively: Many people are so fixated on what they want to say that they hardly listen to the opponent while arguing. It is when you look and listen carefully that you can observe the flaws and weaknesses in his stance. Besides, it could also be an avenue to hear something new and helpful.

7. Study Your Opponent: Listen attentively and know their strengths, belief system, values, and weaknesses. With this, you can appeal to their core values. You can also turn their arguments back to them, leveraging on their faults.

8. Be Ready to Concede a Good Point: Be sure to argue reasonably, not just for the sake of arguments. Admit and acknowledge all valid points that your opponent makes. To look reasonable and have the upper hand, outweigh it with another case. With this, you will appear reasonable.

On the other hand, we will also discuss some interesting things to watch out for and avoid while arguing.

Don't

1. Get personal: Avoid attacking your opponent's lifestyle, integrity, honesty, etc. You are arguing on an issue, not their personality. Besides, avoid retaliating if the other party attacks you. It brings out your maturity and makes you reasonable.

2. Get Distracted: While arguing, it is easy to go off on a tangent. Your opponent might bring in extraneous ideas to counter your point. Make sure you are firm, and you stay on course.

3. Introduce Weak Points in Your Arguments: It is a good idea to focus on your strong points and leave out weak ones. Build on your strong points and make it very convincing so that your opponent will not be able to refute. Weaker arguments give your opponent the chance to weaken your entire case.

HOW TO WIN ARGUMENTS USING HUMAN PSYCHOLOGY

Arguments are pretty frustrating as it comes with an overwhelming need to be heard and receive confirmation. Whatever the point of the argument, whether politics, religion, tribe, etc., no one likes the experience and sense of not gaining the upper hand.

For many people out there who can't seem to find their way around winning argument, psychology has a way out. These tricks will help you even if you are not good at debating. It will make people and your opponent see reason with your side of the matter.

1. Allow Your Opponent to Explain Their Thoughts First

Be sure to arm yourself with open-ended questions that prompt them to explain their ideas and thought process. Before you can have a successful argument, you need to understand your opponent, their thinking patterns and their beliefs about the whole discussion. Be sure not to interrupt them. Let them say everything they need to as they will more likely pay more attention to your rebuttals as well.

2. Mirror Their Body language

This should be done tactically as you shouldn't be too obvious about it. Mirroring is a subtle way to gain your opponent's trust, which increases the chance of them paying attention to you. As subtly as you can, mimic their body language; cross your leg if they are crossing theirs too. However, be smart and not repeat every movement they make. The key is to appear as natural as possible otherwise you will seem as if you are mocking them

"Mirroring builds agreement; you can often head off potential trouble by establishing a strong basis of nonverbal agreement before the real negotiating begins," Nick Morgan.

3. Maintain Eye Contact When You Start Conversation

Be sure to maintain your gaze when your opponent starts talking. Psychology has established that this can weaken your opponent's persuasiveness. With this, you automatically have the upper hand when dishing out your points to counter theirs. Once they start talking again, be sure to make eye contact.

4. Repeat What You Think the Argument is About

Always try and paraphrase what you believe their ideas and points are (as judged from what was said) before dishing out your counterpoints. With this, you build trust because it is an indication that you have been following what they are saying, rather than waiting for them to finish talking, so you can get your points out. If you want to gain your opponent's trust, making your argument persuasive comes easily.

5. Acknowledge their Points

Before you start presenting your arguments, be sure to tell your opponents that you agree with their points. If possible, give them the reason you do. With this, you have encouraged your opponent to listen to your position as well when you dish your arguments out.

6. Know Your Facts

Be very sure you know what you are talking about even before you start talking. Bear in mind that there is a high possibility that the opposite party may ask you to expand or build on some points. You will just look like a fool if you can't explain yourself. Be sure you know your arguments like the back of your hand before presenting them. If you can't expand your points, there is a big chance of losing.

7. Keep Your Voice Down

The last thing you want to do is raise your voice. This will make the entire argument seems like a fight, which will prevent you from arguing reasonably.

With a calm, cool, and composed voice, your opponent will be more at ease of trusting you. This has a high capacity of getting people to consider your point.

8. Identify Common Ground

Throughout arguing, it is essential to keep the atmosphere positive. Keep the dos and don'ts above in mind. Let your opponents know about his/her points that you agree with.

This will likely make them listen to things you do not agree on and might make them consider your angle.

Getting into an argument can be intimidating especially for people who don't like confrontation. However, there are subtle ways of improving your arguing skills and making your points persuasive. While you might not necessarily win an argument with these tricks, you will undoubtedly get people to listen and consider your point of view more.

With this, your confidence increases and you can confront and persuade anyone.

CHAPTER 14:

DETECTING LIES AND DECEPTION

"Every violation of truth is not only a sort of suicide in the liar but is a stab in the health of human society."(Ralph Waldo Emerson, 1803 – 1888,American Essayist)

Is someone lying to you? You do not need to take a criminology class or be a high-class FBI profiler to be able to detect deception. However, detecting lying and deception is a skill many people are yet to learn.

At best, the chances of detecting a lie are 50/50, just like the toss of a coin. You could, however, develop yourself to put the odds of detecting deception in your favor. You could grow up and establish tips to identify lies with accuracy as much as 90%.

This part of the chapter will be divided into three sections:

Part 1: Have a model

Part 2: Search for clues that vary from model behavior and show lying signals

Part 3: Dig more profoundly for the truth if you feel you are being lied to

PART 1: THE MODEL

The model is like the baseline or ideal behavior of the person in normal situations. In other words, how they sound, talk, and react when they have no reason to lie. This is a crucial part of the process of detecting deception.

In establishing the model process, ask questions that the person would not want to lie about. You could ask about their favorite meal or their favorite movie. During the process, be sure to pay attention to how they talk, their facial expressions, and their choice of words. Start with a physical model.

Part 1a: The Physical Model

Here, you will have to take note of all the physical characteristics shown during the conversation. You can approach it by breaking it down into various body segments.

Be sure to take note of:

- The face

- The head

- The torso

- The arms and hands

- The legs and feet

Take note of the various body parts. During the conversation, what are they doing with their body parts? Are they continually touching their sleeve, their face, or rubbing their arm? Are they tapping their feet? What is the frequency? These are the models and characteristics you should watch out for. Hence, when the model part is over, you will look out for deviations from these behaviors.

Now that you have an idea of their physical behavior when not stressed let us get on to the next model.

Part 1b: The Audio Model

During the audio model, take note of their vocal pitch and how they sound during a normal conversation, a situation where they have no reason to lie. Be sure to take note of their tone, volume, speech patterns, word choices, word fillers, and gestures.

It doesn't stop at the physical and audio model as we need to establish an emotional model as well. This has to do with developing a model of when they are anxious, excited, or nervous about an issue. This is the weakness of "lie detectors." They judge someone as lying whereas he was just emotional or passionate about the subject of discussion.

Be sure not to pass on this step, so you do not wrongly assume someone is lying when they are not.

Part 1c: Emotional Model

This part also involves asking questions. The difference, however, is that you will ask questions that will either get the person upset or excited. This will give you a physical and audio model of them in an emotional state.

You could ask about politics, a day they will never forget, what caused their divorce or the loss of a kid, their favorite sports teams, or anything they are passionate about to get them excited. Ask them something that will likely upset them. The lost of a brother, sister or a family member, their medical issue, etc. will make a good question (however, exercise caution).

With this, you get to observe and search for deviations in their behavior in comparison to the model you took of their "normal" behavior. For instance, when they talked about their favorite movie, their voice was filled with affection, more energy, and movement.

Also, it is likely when you asked about an issue that makes them upset, they clenched their fist, might have stiffened up, or changed the pitch of their tone.

These are the baselines for the various conditions. This is their "ideal" models, whether excited or upset. Be sure to take note of variations and similarities in the baseline you took.

Model Complete

This is the end of the model process. The idea is to make you understand the person under normal conditions when they have no reason to lie.

PART 2: LOOK FOR DIFFERENCES AND LYING CUES

In establishing if someone is lying or not, you should consider deviations from the models found above.

If while establishing the model, they gestured a lot, but the hands are steady, there is a chance they might be lying.

If they are now clenching their fist, which they didn't do during the model stage, that is suspicious.

Count it as a red flag as well if their pitch is suddenly high, low, or hesitant.

These variations are clues you should watch out for. In addition to these variations, there are lying cues you should watch out for. These cues are huge red flags that have been established to reveal if a person is lying or not.

- When the facial emotion contradicts the words said

- Nodding 'no' when saying 'yes' and vice versa

- Grooming and other self-soothing behaviors

- Touching any part of the face like the nose or mouth

- Distancing or blocking behavior like touching the mouth or ears when speaking

- Long pauses and excessive use of filler words like hmms or ums when talking

- Excessive phrases like "to be honest with you..." or starting a statement with honestly...

- They appear to be thinking really hard

In the process of the conversation, you might have taken note of one or two red flags or clues. Take note of this.

Part 2b: Seek out Clusters

A cluster is when you have three or more variations, red flags, or lying cues. As you converse, take note of the red flags and see if any of them fit as clusters.

If you have a cluster for any response, that is an indication of lying. Although, it might also be that the person is uncomfortable about a part of the conversation, or hiding information. Whatever the case may be, you should examine this further.

PART 3: PRESS FURTHER

If during your discussion or rather, investigation, you find clusters. You shouldn't just leave it. You should press further and dig more in-depth, however, what do you do exactly in this case?

You have got to decide what matters. Every day, we experience lies and deception in one form or the other from friends, co-workers, and family members. However, many of this doesn't matter. If it is not essential, you can choose to overlook it.

If it is however important to you, and you need confirmation if they are lying or not, you should press further.

In pressing further, ask open-ended questions like "could you please tell me more about......?"or "when you said... what do you mean?"

With this, they get to talk more, giving you a chance to observe and establish your facts.

On a final note, you can suddenly present them with a question and watch their reaction. If you come at them suddenly, you throw them off and destabilize them so that they have no choice but to let out some truth.

This process will help to establish your lie detection skills. Do not be disappointed if you don't find yourself being too skillful with this. A talent this worthwhile doesn't come on a silver platter. Over the years, there has been research into lying and deception which are common human behaviors. While we understand that the above might take a while to master, some clear signs indicate that someone is lying.

Bear in mind that at times, some people lie to protect other people's feelings. If a woman asks a man, for instance, "am I fat?" And the man responded with a smile and said, "no you are not." That could be a white lie meant to protect the other party. There are, however, severe cases of lying (covering up a crime for instance) in which the time to establish a baseline and model presented above might not present itself.

Over the years, researchers have strived to bring forth various ways of detecting lies. Although it is not very simple to tell if someone is lying, there are a few indicators.

SIMPLE SIGNS TO DETECT IF SOMEONE IS LYING

Just as we established previously, trusting your instinct is primal inidentifying a lie. In identifying a lie, people focus on body language and some behavioral and physical signs that show lying. Constant fidgeting, shifty eyes, and avoiding eye contact are standard signs that you are dealing with a liar.

Although body language cues could indicate that someone is lying, research has shown that many of these behaviors don't have to do with lying. For instance, psychologist Howard Ehrlichman's research in eye movement revealed that eye movement does not necessarily mean that someone is lying. He suggested that shifting eyes could mean one is in deep thought or trying to tap into the long-term memory.

With this in mind, body language can be a terrific tool in detecting lies. However, it is essential to understand the particular signal you are going with.

What are the signals associated with lying?

1. They provide excessive detail

A liar is never comfortable with silence, hence; they supply more unnecessary detail than needed. You will get more information that you requested. Sometimes, just staying quiet might inconvenience the liar, thus they try to fill the silence with details to support the claim. This is usually in a bid to convince you and themselves to accept their deception. Besides, to get more time to put their thoughts together, liars will often repeat a phrase many times.

2. They try desperately to be still

While it might seem strange, being very still might be a pointer that a person is deceptive. This is because the person is trying to hide tension by minimizing their body movements. Hence, you see the person pull their legs and arms towards the body, all because of pressure.

Think about it, people are generally relaxed and free in a normal situation, with the tendency to move body parts and express themselves freely. However, when they are trying to hide something fishy, they might be rigid.

3. Their body language contradicts what they are saying

Some people tell you they are fine yet their body expressions and language say otherwise. At times, these people are even lying to themselves. In other words, their feelings don't match their words. Think of it as someone who frowns after saying, "I'm fine." – something is off. Also, pay attention to someone who shakes their head up and down while replying 'no.'

4. Changes in breathing

Heavy breathing or a change in breathing pattern is a sign of nervousness. It could also be an indication that someone is hiding information. As a reflex, when people lie, they breathe heavily because lying triggers a change in blood flow and the heart rate. At times, someone who is lying might have trouble speaking as a result of the drying out of the mucous membrane in some parts of the mouth.

5. Change in patterns of eye movement

It is often said that the eyes are the window to the soul. This applies to lying as well, although you have to be careful. In using the eyes to detect lying, it is not about the direction of sight but a change in the direction. Hence, in trying hard to recollect information, some people might look up and look down while lying. This could be the opposite for others.

Be attentive to a change in eye movement. It is a strong indication of lying. However, be sure to know the person's model first (as explained in the previous section). This is why this tactic is suited to people you are familiar with. A universal basis is that people who are lying do look at the door – because this is an unconscious escape route for them.

6. Making excessive pauses

Making an unusual pause is a clear sign of lying. This is a tactic to buy time to organize their thoughts or construct a storyline to sell to you. In trying to detect if someone is lying, be sure to take note of these pauses. They often hesitate and appear to be thinking hard to ensure that their stories have a flow and are believable.

7. They fidget

Fidgeting, without a doubt, is a sign of negative energy. Experienced liars (except psychopaths) often fall victim of this as they are not sure that you will buy their story. Hence, in a bid to let go of that nervous energy, they stroke their hair, play with their hands, and tap their feet, and display other unusual signs. Shuffling the feet, for instance, is conventional negative energy associated with lying. The feet are unstable because the liar is uneasy and the body is trying to get away!

8. Watch for changes in language

Watch out for distancing language as liars might try to distance themselves from the lie. Watch for the use of pronouns as they speak. For instance, "I killed your chicken" could become "I killed the chicken." This is usually an effort of the liar to distance themselves from the subject of discussion.

9. Pay attention to the word "no."

How does the person say the word no? Do they say no and look away? Do they say no and close their eyes briefly? Pause for a while and say no? Do they drag out the word and say nooooooo? Pay attention to all these clues.

10. Repeating the question

While many would want to make sure they heard you right, a liar could just be stalling for time. He might be trying to dig deeper and figure out how much you know. Pay attention to this alongside other clues on the list.

Assembling all the Clues

For emphasis sake, do not rush into conclusions. Be sure to know and understand what forms the usual and necessary behavior of this person in question. The signs of lying discussed above only make sense concerning the person's normal behavior.

If you are dealing with a victim of ADHD who fidgets easily, you can rule out some of these signs as lying indicators. Psychopaths as well do not show most of these signs as they hardly feel remorse about lying.

Final Thoughts on How to Tell if Someone is Lying

In conclusion, the reality is that there are no general and sure-fire signs that you can look at to confirm that someone is lying. All the indicators and pointers that researchers have gathered over the years are just clues that can help reveal who is hiding something or not.

With this in mind, the next time you are trying to authenticate a person's information, don't be so focused on the signs of lying. Be sure to train yourself to pay attention to subtle behaviors that show deception. If possible, add pressure to the individual so that telling a lie becomes mentally hard, for instance, ask him to narrate the incidence in reverse.

On a final note, as it's been emphasized, be sure to follow your gut!

CONCLUSION

There is a wealth of information about the people we interact with on a daily basis that can tell us who they truly are and what they are currently thinking about as we interact with them. The challenge, however, is how to master the skills required to read this information.

Analyzing people may seem like a daunting task, but even if you are not an undercover security agent, you can develop the skills required for reading people. For many people, they recoil when they hear the term "human psychology." It sounds too complicated a subject to be understood. But in this book, I have taken the time to present the skills to read basic human psychology in a very simple way that anyone can understand. If you begin to apply what you have studied in this book, you will see how it is relatively easy to understand people and see them in a different light. It is like lifting a veil that has been covering your eyes for a long time.

I encourage you to take the advice of dropping all prejudices if you must make any headway in accurately reading people. Equally, empathizing with others will greatly improve your chances of solidifying your business or personal relationship with them.

If you can practice these key lessons for a few weeks, you will notice a significant improvement in your career, business, and personal relationships. There is no point in studying how to analyze people without practicing it. That is why I encourage you to study this book more than once. Make it your companion until you have mastered your people-reading skills to a comfortable degree. Your particular scenario may not have been mentioned in this book, but you can always apply the tips to whatever peculiar situation you find yourself.

Finally, be sure to be discreet and "covert" about this whole reading people business. If you make it obvious that you are trying to read people, you most probably are not going to get any meaningful results. In other words, you must first master the body language of being secretive before you can effectively analyze people. After all, you cannot demonstrate what you do not have yourself.

Expect rapid positive changes in your career as you implement the ideas in this book.

REFERENCES

1. Dimitruis, J. &Mazzarella, M. Reading people: How to understand people and predict their behavior - anytime, anyplace. Retrieved February 8, 2019, from http://edition.cnn.com/books/beginnings/9807/reading .people.cnn/index.html

2. Bariso, J. An FBI agent shares 9 secrets to reading people. Retrieved February 9, 2019, from https://www.inc.com/justin-bariso/an-fbi-agents-9-ways-to-read-people.html

3. Cherry, K. Top 10 nonverbal communication tips. Retrieved February 9, 2019 from https://www.verywellmind.com/top-nonverbal-communication-tips-2795400

4. Lewis, J. Four types of business personalities. Retrieved February 9, 2019 from https://smallbusiness.chron.com/four-types-business-personalities-26162.html

5. Hubbard, R. Communicating with the four personality types. Retrieved February 9, 2019 from https://www.iidmglobal.com/expert_talk/expert-talk-categories/managing-people/staff_communication/id23383.html

6. Human metrics Inc. Determining other people's personality. Retrieved February 14, 2019 from http://www/humanmetrics.com/personality/how-to-determine-other-peoples-type

7. Beckman Institute for Advanced Science and Technology. (2012). Science reveals the power of a handshake. Science Daily. Retrieved February 8, 2019 from www.sciencedaily.com/releases/2012/10/121019141300.htm

8. Clarke, G. The top 10 tips for the ultimate power handshake. Retrieved February 8, 2019 from https://www.europeanceo.com/business-and-management/top-10-tips-for-the-power-handshake/

9. Brooks, L. The Power of a Handshake. Retrieved February 8, 2019 from http://careerskillet.org/the-power-of-a-handshake/

10. White, J. 6 Techniques for building rapport that will help you connect with anyone. Retrieved February 10, 2019

from https://www.learning-mind.com/building-rapport-techniques/

11. Wood, C. 12 Body language signals only the best salespeople can read. Retrieved February 10, 2019 from https://www.nutshell.com/blog/body-language-signals-sales/

12. Universal Class. Understanding body language in business. Retrieved February 14, 2019 fromhttps://www.universalclass.com/articles/business/understanding-body-language-in-business.htm

13. Goman, C. K. 10 Powerful body language tips. Retrieved February 14, 2019 fromhttps://www.amanet.org/training/articles/10-powerful-body-language-tips.aspx

14. Science of People. Office body language: 5 cues you must know. Retrieved February 14, 2019 from https://www.scienceofpeople.com/see-easily-can-master-office-body-language/

15. Farrington, J. How to deal effectively with objections. Retrieved February 9, 2019 from http://saleshq.monster.com/training/articles/230-how-to-deal-effectively-with-objections

16. Connick, W. How to handle objections in 6 easy steps.

Retrieved February 9, 2019 from https://www.thebalancecareers.com/how-to-handle-objections-in-six-easy-steps-2917496/b

17. Kyle M. 3 scientific tips to detect lying. Retrieved February 10, 2019 from https://www.realmenrealstyle.com/lie-detection/

18. Kendra, C. How to recognize the signs that someone is lying. Retrieved February 10, 2019 from https://www.verywellmind.com/how-to-tell-if-someone-is-lying-2795917

19. Bett & Kate M. The three elements of Charisma: Presence. Retrieved February 10, 2019 from https://www.artofmanliness.com/articles/the-3-elements-of-charisma-presence/

20. Bet t& Kate M. The three elements of Charisma: Power. Retrieved February 10, 2019 from https://www.artofmanliness.com/articles/the-3-elements-of-charisma-power/

21. Bett & Kate M. The three elements of Charisma: Warmth. Retrieved February 10, 2019 from https://www.artofmanliness.com/articles/the-3-elements-of-charisma-warmth/

22. Fremont. How to read body language – revealing the

secret behind non verbal clues. Retrieved February 11, 2019 from https://fremont.edu/how-to-read-body-language-revealing-the-secrets-behind-common-nonverbal-cues/

23. Kendra, C. Understanding Body language and facial expressions. Retrieved February 11, 2019 from https://www.verywellmind.com/understand-body-language-and-facial-expressions-4147228

24. Brian, T. 6 Nonverbal communication examples to increase sales. Retrieved February 11, 2019 from https://www.briantracy.com/blog/sales-success/6-ways-to-use-body-language-to-get-what-you-want-nonverbal-communication/

25. Cara, W. 12 body Language signals only the best salesmen can read. Retrieved February 11, 2019 from https://www.nutshell.com/blog/body-language-signals-sales/

www.ingramcontent.com/pod-product-compliance
Lightning Source LLC
Chambersburg PA
CBHW030517210326
41597CB00013B/935